Urban Joy

Happy Reading

Beverly

it has been a divine connection in meeting you. :)

Robin Medley-Israel

First printing, November, 2013

ISBN-13: 978-0-9859255-7-4
ISBN-10: 0-9859255-7-4

Published by:

ThomasMax Publishing
P.O. Box 250054
Atlanta, GA 30325
www.thomasmax.com

Urban Joy

by Robin A. Medley-Israel

ThomasMax

TM

Your Publisher
For The 21st Century

~A Word from the Publisher~

When Robin Medley first called ThomasMax Publishing years ago at the recommendation of a mutual friend, it seemed like a "here-we-go-again" moment. We get lots of calls from people who have plans to write books and want to know how it works to get it published. Little did we know then that Robin wasn't your everyday, run-of-the-mill, "I have a book in me" kind of person.

Just a few short weeks before publication, she called again to inquire about details before researching some other possible publishing avenues. She then returned to us and said she was ready to work with ThomasMax.

One of the stipulations was that we were to edit her work. That's something we do often. But once I began the task of reading her story, I found myself wondering just how much editing I should be doing. Here was a woman who had spoken to God, to whom God had given instruction to write. The book was formatted well short of perfection. I felt that if God instructed her to write this book, how much did I dare to change? Ultimately Robin put my mind at ease in giving me latitude to change as I saw fit. Ultimately, too, I told her if we changed something that in some way altered her intent, she was free to tell us to change it back.

This is a one-of-a-kind book. In the world of books, testimonies are frequent and life stories are abundant. Motivational, preachy texts are commonplace. This one, however, is different even though it comprises all of these elements. I doubt that you will never read another book that contains these similar characteristics in such a raw, candid way. Robin reveals details about her life that many would take great pains to hide. Perhaps that's why I do believe that God inspired her to write this book, and why we at ThomasMax are proud to be a part of it.

Lee Clevenger, President, ThomasMax Publishing

~Dedication~

In Loving Memory of my grand baby,
Elijah Witt.
"I know you are in the arms of the Lord."

~About the Author~

Robin is an extraordinary woman who is known for her smile, laughter and singing. To know her is to love her. Her joy, caring, giving and counseling have touched the hearts of many. Even as a child, she had an advanced sense that enabled her to grasp wisdom and give counsel to people beyond her age. Some called her an "Old Soul." It came natural for her to discern beyond the surface of a matter and quickly get to the root of it. In some instances, she could actually see and or perceive the future. Robin's life has had many twists and turns. Many adverse circumstances were dealt to her from an infancy to the present. However, her resilience through it all is recognized and felt by all who know her.

Robin was born in Camden, NJ, and raised by her late mother Barbara. She was married for twenty-six years and had the privilege to birth and raise two beautiful daughters. The first born is Angela and the baby girl is Stephenie. She went to Rutgers University for two years and majored in Accounting. After experiencing a supernatural intervention, her course of life changed. Robin professed the Christian faith and her purpose in life became clearer. Robin went into full-time ministry and served under Dr. James Treadwell for twenty-four years. During that time, she attended TEIA School of Ministry, was graduated and became licensed and ordained to minister. She has served as a Christian Academy School Administrator to grade levels K-12. She also served as an on staff Pastor/Counselor, Ministerial Board Chairman, and Board of Stewards member. After serving under Dr. Treadwell, she supported her husband by relocating to North Carolina to start a ministry. It was at this point that, ***Urban Joy*** was birthed.

~ *Acknowledgments* ~

The Lord was gracious to inspire me to write ***Urban Joy*** and I thank Him. I thank all of my family and friends who have shown me much love and support. I would be remiss if I did not also thank those of you who were merciless, selfish, unkind, and loveless. God has used your deeds to bring me to a level of forgiveness, maturity and joy that I would never have experienced if it wasn't for you.

~Foreword~

I must start by saying that I really enjoyed writing this book. The experience has been an honor as well as humbling. ***Urban Joy*** was written during a time in my life when I had to face heart-wrenching, life-changing, adverse circumstances. The book was written during a time when I desperately needed something to divert my attention in order to preserve my sanity and stability. My inspiration to focus on joy was divinely and strategically orchestrated. As a result, the quality of my living has been bumped to First Class.

To prepare you for this life changing experience, please, before reading this book, ask yourself the following questions: Why am I reading a book about joy? Am I a joyful person no matter my circumstance? How often do I consider joy during my daily routine? How often do I consider joy during transacting business? Do I believe that joy has its moments, or do I believe that joy should be experienced every hour of the day? Do I think to be joyous is a personality trait only found in certain people? The answers to all of these questions and more will be revealed during your experience of reading ***Urban Joy***.

Urban Joy is a book with many treasures inside; treasures that will enrich your life **completely. Expect a *paradigm shift.* Be ready for *a change in perception, a change in your point of view* and *a change in how you see things in your everyday living*.** Anticipate fulfilling your purpose in this life with sheer pleasure. Look forward to the windows of your dreams being wiped clean as the sunshine of joy lightens the path of fulfilling them. ***Urban Joy*** will permeate your gifts and talents as you uniquely make a mark in your home, work place, community, and even the world regardless of your hindrances, weaknesses, and mistakes. John Maxwell (Renowned Inspirational author and Pastor) says, "No matter what a person's past may have been, his future is spotless. You can begin pursuing your dream today!" In essence ***Urban Joy*** enables you to competently and triumphantly pursue your dreams from start to finish.

We all have been created with the capability to dream even if for whatever reason we do not allow those dreams to come to fruition. We all have a unique calling in life. We all have been given gifts and talents that are beautiful assets to our everyday living. However, harsh realities and adversities tend to be the reason as to why our God-given beauty and abilities fade away like a mist in the wind. They tragically die silent deaths. It doesn't matter who we are or our circumstance, we all have a running chance at being extraordinary. ***Urban Joy*** is a catalyst in making that happen. "... The extraordinary is not the birthright of a chosen and privileged few, but of all people, even the humblest. That is my one certainty: we are all the manifestation of the divinity of God." -- Paulo Coelho (best-selling Portuguese language author).

There are many who have found a place of contentment in their life. Things are going well for them in their relationships, career, and spirituality. This book may be a confirmation for them. However, there is a larger percentage of people who struggle on a daily basis to be happy. They struggle daily with anger, frustration, depression, grief, resentment, jealousy, hatred, disappointment, bitterness, victimization and such like. As you journey through reading ***Urban Joy*** with an open mind, you will experience a newness of heart. Your ineffective ways of handling the many issues in life will be debilitated. In this book there are examples and effective methods that will empower you to maintain your stance of living a happy and joyful life despite the circumstance. Owning the revelation of ***Urban Joy*** will position you to stand above hindering forces. This type joy will strengthen and encourage you in your journey to be able to withstand the tests and trials of life with a calming smile on the inside.

~ Table of Contents ~

~ *The Eve of My Beginning* ~

I opened my eyes into this world as a bastard child, but to make it sound a little more pleasant, I was born as a "Love Child." From what I was told, instead of the celebration of life, there was much controversy concerning my birth. I was not planned. I was seemingly considered to be a mistake. My mother went through much to keep my biological father a secret. In some family circles, because of the controversy, even as a baby I was not accepted. Unlike most American babies, I don't have baby pictures or happy stories surrounding my birth to reflect upon. However, my mother showered me with love and affection. She endlessly hugged and loved on me while shielding me from the truth.

As a shielded vessel, my beginning into the path of joy well over four decades ago has been quite interesting, to say the least. To paint a picture on the canvas of your mind, every morning in elementary school I remember standing with my right hand over my heart singing, "My country 'tis of thee, sweet land of liberty of thee I sing….." I was oblivious to the true meaning of what I was singing. Yes, I lived in the great U.S. of A., but in a place far from the Grand Canyon, the beautiful deep blue shores of Hawaii, Niagara Falls and the breath-taking Biltmore Estate. It was a special place called the "Ghetto." My *Oh beautiful for spacious skies* stood in stark contrast to others. There, our liberty and beauty were quite different. We seemed to march to our own beat of life.

As an African American, I was born and raised in Camden, New Jersey, the home of the famous Campbell Soup Company. The success and reputation of Campbell Soup's products and the wholesome image projected through their commercials was not enough to turn *Time* magazine from listing Camden, out of 35,000 cities and towns in the United States, as being one of the worst cities in which to raise a family. Growing up in Camden, I witnessed the reasons for this firsthand. It was normal for me to see just about every self-destructive addiction known. There were the painted faces of the provocative "drag queens" and prostitutes parading down Broadway performing a daily show of competition to appease the sexual cravings of every "Tom,

Dick and Harry," their acts openly in the alleys or behind mailboxes day time and night time, men in their vehicles parked off to the side masturbating after leaving the X-Rated bars on the Boulevard, the discarded heroin needles and condoms that washed alongside the curb on a rainy day, the exchanging of drugs and money around the clock. I was disturbed by the arguments and fights due to drunkenness, and the cuts in my hand and foot that had to be stitched up in the emergency ward (each time caused by the broken glass of alcoholic beverage bottles thrown on the streets). As I walked to school, I remember stepping over the colorful landscaping of trash, soiled disposable diapers, feminine products and garbage that took the place of plants, bushes and shrubs on some streets.

I was surrounded by dysfunction due to poor choices and misfortune. I grew up living around these things but I was immune to my environment. It was all I knew. My little friends and I played "Hop Scotch," "Double Dutch," "1, 2, 3, Red Light" and "Hide and Seek" like any other city kids, laughing, playing and running after the ice cream truck. We scurried for change just to get to the candy store every day as well as using board game chips instead of coins to empty some unfortunate business owner's bubblegum machine.

In the Ghetto, the media always focused on the bad things that happened, like drive-by shootings. However, they never focused on those who would be so generous by giving us drive-by concerts. The woofers on the natives' cars were so big and loud that the vibration of the base could be felt two blocks down. At any given time, you would see the natives breaking it down, dancing to the music on the sidewalk or street corners like a scene from a Ghetto "Who Ville." Outlanders perceived the Ghetto to be bad. They would lock their doors as they drove by. However, we, the natives, had an understanding about how things were. I remember neighbors helping neighbors when in need. My mom would empty her freezer many times to give to those who did not have food even while struggling herself to make ends meet.

I was single-handedly raised by my late mother, Barbara. Mommy did her best to love and care for me and my siblings, Yolanda and Eric. Like many single-parent homes in the urban neighborhoods, my family at one point, depended on welfare. Mommy worked hard to get us out of the Social Service system. She tried many jobs to support our family. When I was seven years old, Mommy started dating a Puerto Rican co-worker she met at one of those jobs. At that time, the Black Panthers and the Latinos were feuding because a young girl got raped in an alley. On the street, it was not said but it was understood that Blacks and Latinos shouldn't mix. Uncomfortable by his presence, my brother and sister told their friends that he was the TV repairman when he came to visit. However, one day, that TV repairman never left. I remember my brother, sister and I getting in trouble with Mom several times for ducking down to hide in the back seat of our car when her Puerto Rican friend would ride with us through our neighborhood. Despite our embarrassment, he and Mom eventually married.

As time moved on, Eric and Yolanda were old enough to move on with their lives. However, I was too young and he became the only father figure in the home to help mommy to raise me. Consequently, he gained my trust by doing family things with us, like playing a game of jacks with Mom and me from time to time, eating dinner with us at the dinner table, and going to church. He was nice to me and always played with me. I had begun to feel a sense of wholesomeness about the normalcy of my new family structure.

Yet as I began to get older and physically develop, my stepfather's interest changed from that of being a father to something shockingly different. At the age of eleven, my breasts developed pretty large for my age. He woke me one morning calling for me to come into my mother's room. She was at work. Still rubbing my eyes trying to wake up, he told me to sit in my mother's big chair. As I sat, still not quite alert, he began to talk to me. While talking, he coasted his way into telling me that he could do things to my breast that a father should not want to do with his daughter. With a blanket draped over his bottom half and no shirt on, he tried to convince me that it would be good for me. I was so shocked by his approach that I could no longer speak. I felt glued to my mother's chair. His words caused my ears to ring. I just nodded my head out of respect as he asked me mind boggling questions.

His brother (visiting from Newark, NJ) calling his name at the end of the stairs interrupted him from sexually assaulting me that morning. That interruption helped me to break away and run to my room. My emotions shifted from being shocked to confused, and then angry. For the first time in my life, I remember a dark feeling of hate entering my heart, removing all my feelings of love and respect for him. I no longer saw him as a father, his cover was blown. I saw him for who he was, a perverted, sick, poor excuse of a man who subtly took camp in my mother's house.

I did not tell anyone of his advances towards me. I had to secretly fight to protect myself. I did not tell anyone because I did not want my six-foot-two, muscular, Paul Bunyan of a brother ruining his life by killing that Chihuahua of a man. In my mind, he could have been a stunt double for the "Yo Quiero Taco Bell" commercials. My brother would literally grab his friends up by their necks and lift them off the ground if they looked at me crooked. There is no telling what he would have done to a man that he didn't like. I also did not want to chance telling my mother. I had seen her hurt deeply by people many times and I could not bear to see her hurt any more. I was hoping that this perverted microfiber of a man would go away and never come back. Unfortunately, he did not go away.

From the age of eleven, my house was no longer a home. It became a battlefield until I moved out at the age of twenty. I would no longer let him nicely get close to me. In my younger days, I would go to bed early when Mommy wouldn't be home to foil his opportunity to approach me. At times, he would take long showers and open my bedroom door and stand there for a while with nothing on but a towel. I pretended to be asleep. Each time it looked like he got more courage to come over to my bed to mess with me, Mommy would put her key in the door, causing him to run out of my room. As I got older, many nights Mommy would be home resting in her bedroom, he would leave their room and quietly come behind me and repeatedly rub my breasts as my back would be turned washing the dishes. I would elbow him, scream out, "*Mom!!!"* and also threaten to tell. He would back off of me. One time, he had the audacity to say, "Tell 'er, she's not gonna belief ju." I was repulsed and disgusted by his presence. He always walked around without a shirt on even when my friends would come to visit. He obsessively rubbed his neck and chest, like he was mental, until his skin looked blood red. I thought he subconsciously was trying to rub off all of his filthy thoughts and deeds.

I ignored and resisted him. My body grew fast and being 5'6"-5'7," athletically built and big-boned, I could put up a little fight. I know if I was a tiny girl, he would have had his way with me. I became obnoxious hoping to slap the taste out of his mouth for wanting me. He physically shoved and man handled me on many occasions, sometimes with a sick giggle, as if he got some demented pleasure from my resistance. At times, he would restrain me by holding me with his hands cupped around my breast. Every time he tried to mishandle me, I would fight back. I would scratch, punch, kick, elbow, bite, or hit him with some object nearby. One time when I was home alone with him, frustrated because of my resistance, he kicked me down a few flights of stairs. One other time he threw me out of my mother's house with no coat in the dead of winter. I yelled and banged on the door loudly so that my next door neighbors could hear me. He eventually opened the door and did not bother me anymore for a while. Annoyed by my hate and not consenting, he began to start telling lies on me. I had to defend myself often. One time, I was greeted at the front door by my mother striking me with a long black umbrella because of a lie he told. I remember disrespectfully screaming, "He lied," from the pit of my stomach as I ran to my room. The umbrella didn't hurt more than her believing him. Mommy did not come after me for screaming at her. I believe it is because her motherly instincts told her that I was telling the truth. We never talked about it. A couple of times, I had been sent to bed without eating dinner because I would not bow my head nor close my eyes at the dinner table when he hypocritically prayed the grace. I eventually found reasons not to eat dinner with them.

He would try and manipulate my mother by telling her that he loved me like a daughter and he didn't understand why I didn't treat him like a father. I saw straight through his twisted, deceitful words. The combination of my thoughts of hatred, disgust, repulse and resentment guarded my heart from being manipulated. My mom being oblivious to his sickness, thought I had an attitude problem and could not understand what was wrong with her ordinarily loving, sweet child. Unfortunately, my mother concluded that I was jealous of their relationship. When Mom thought I was asleep, frustrated, she would vent the misunderstanding to her friends on the phone. A number of times I would hear her call me a hussy and heifer. I did not take it to heart because I knew that she was only speaking out of her frustration. I ignored what I suffered to spare my mother from what I considered to be worse: the horrible, hurtful, pedophilia intentions of her nasty, sick husband.

Subconsciously I knew that regardless of what had been dealt to me, I had been given a life with challenges to make something of it. As I got older, I spent less and less time at home. I immersed myself in school activities such as volleyball, cheerleading and became more social with my peers. In high school, I also made it a hobby to look for things to laugh about. I was captain of the cheerleading squad from ninth to twelfth grade. I showed off leading our squads to march with the band in our beautiful purple and gold uniforms. “Drum Line” is in my movie collection, solely because it captures the memories of my glorious gratification of marching with an outstanding band. Camden High was known nationally in those days. Their football and basketball teams were undefeated. The scouts flooded our games. I walked the halls with Milton Wagner and became friends with Billy Thompson. Both were drafted by the LA Lakers.

With the bleachers packed and the exhilarating rumbling of the drums, I led pep rallies and made up a song for the huge crowd of Panther fans to sing. In the midst of the brilliant colors of purple, gold and remnants of white, my singing sounded so good to this one guy that he screamed from the bleachers, “Sing it, Diana!!!” (referring to Dianna Ross). In my mind a good comparison of the Panther fans thunderous applause and hype, would be the spectators in the movie “Gladiator” when Maximus stepped out into the Roman stadium. The roar of the crowd and cheering was exhilarating.

I had the opportunity to travel to different states for our team's tournaments. We proudly paraded around in our purple jackets that signified *Cheerleader* in bright gold letters. As the captain of the cheerleading squad for one of the best basketball teams in the nation, I developed a strong sense of self-confidence and self-esteem. I also felt a sense of pride about the team I represented. I was so enthusiastic about my team that I was elected in my yearbook as having “The Most School Spirit.” Like everything in life, that special time had to come to an end. I graduated with honors in the top thirty of a class of five hundred. The minuscule quantum of days in high school left me with an impactful, concentrated capsule of great memories, in contrast to the scheme of my life to that point.

All during my school days if I was not active in school, I preferred hanging out with my mom, grandparents, cousins and a high-school friend. Looking back, I also stayed in the house watching television a good portion of the time. I grew up snuggling under my mom’s coffee table as I watched my favorite shows. On television, I was attracted to people who lived differently than I did, like in the hit TV shows “Family Affair” and “The Brady Bunch.” The families on these shows appeared to have functional and prosperous lives and I wanted that type of living. I believed that if I gained wealth, I would have a better life. I thought that being rich was comprised of having a lot of materialistic things and money. As a girl, I saw the "bling, bling" ghetto-fabulous image of wearing gold jewelry, long acrylic nails, fancy hair styles, imitation designer clothes and buying bootleg movies. If you asked me, I wanted to be in the movies. I did not want to just look rich, I wanted to be rich. From TV, I only had images. But I really did not have a clue about what it would be like to be rich.

At the age of eighteen, during my last year in high school, I was introduced to a path that transformed the course of my life completely. The end of this path awaited a whole new concept of being rich. During this time of transformation, I was secretly distraught about the dysfunctions in my life. For one, I was forced to live with a perverted, lying stepfather. Secondly, I got pregnant right after losing my virginity to my high school sweetheart (whom I later married). Thirdly, he, respecting the advice of his family, decided that a baby would mess up his future, and so he asked me to get an abortion. He also mentally checked out, admitting that my pregnancy was too much for him to handle. Fourthly, I was emotionally in shambles for the following reasons: he left me with the disparity of dealing with the matter alone, I was upset by his suggestion to abort the baby, and I was very disturbed by the future possibility of my child having a perverted stepfather like I did. Fifthly, I was embarrassed. I felt stupid for toying with the passions of kissing and was not prepared for the serious consequences of having sex. I was horribly disappointed by my thinking that it was okay to do it with my first love because I was certain that I was going to marry him. But in reality, it was not okay. The experience was not as beautiful as I imagined it to be and the results were awful. Lastly, I was hurt to think that the man that I loved, did not want our baby. I did not want my future child to be born in such turmoil, so I thought the decision to abort the baby was best.

The abortion was the worst thing I have done in my life. After that brief moment of hearing my flesh and blood being sucked through a machine, I could not believe I did such a horrible thing. Yes, I signed the consent form after sitting in a cold, dismal room alone crying my eyes out for over an hour. Yes, I had heard of so many others doing it, seemingly, without a problem. However, I was not prepared for the reality of the execution. I was deeply hurt by my actions, emotionally unstable, perplexed, and my mind was overwhelmed and baffled by the thought that I had the right to vacuum away my undeveloped child. I was not mature enough to handle the horror and emotional distress resulting from such an act.

As a young girl, I managed to grow up without my father. I was able to manage through living in a rough environment. I managed to live in a home with a perverted stepfather. I managed to fight when he wanted to physically handle me. I managed through being punished because of the lies of my stepfather. I managed through being called names by a mother who did not understand the drastic change in my attitude. I managed through seeing the young man I fell in love with mentally check out after all that we shared together. However, aborting my baby and hearing it being vacuumed out of my body was the pinnacle of me taking steps to end my life. I was oppressed with the thought of how life always resulted in hurt and pain. For that reason, I concluded that life was not worth living.

I sat at my mother's kitchen table and wrote out different ways of killing myself. I finally decided to digest all of every ten to twelve bottles of prescribed medication in our medicine cabinet. Leaving the death note with remnants of my scattered thoughts of depression, I got up to carry out my devised plan. In that same moment, I encountered a supernatural visitation from God in my mother's kitchen. God intervened by way of an audible voice. He said to me, "If you give your life to me, I will not hurt you." When I heard His voice, I stopped and looked behind me only to see my mother's green stove. Bewildered and depressed, I turned away and continued forward to end my life. When God said it to me again, I knew that it was Him speaking to me because, this time, the words were spoken in my heart. My legs weakened and I fell to my knees. There on my knees, He ministered to my heart.

The hurt of not giving my baby a chance to live, the disparity of my dysfunctional life, and the depression lifted off of me as God ministered to my heart. Immediately, I experienced an overwhelming sense of being cleansed and forgiven. I felt pure love and care after what I had done. A solid foundation of truth that He will never hurt or abandon me brought me to a place of hope and joy that life never afforded me the opportunity to experience. This was the breaking of a day in which the course of my life had transformed. Even though the people and the things around me were the same; I saw life completely differently because I was different. Life was so much brighter because of Him. My heart was full of joy. The eve of my beginning gave way to a new day. The dawning of a richer life was shining bright before me.

At the age of eighteen, my transformation began. All of my perceptions and intent were made new. Even a new perspective of being rich unfurled before me. In precise detail, I had begun to see a prosperous life being more than my girlish dreams. My spiritual walk with Christ sharpened my vision and intellect to discern the truth that where someone lives does not determine the evidence of this type wealth. I could clearly see that we can live in the urban neighborhoods, the suburbs, a mansion or a country trailer home and still be rich. I have come to understand that being rich does not conclude with earthly possessions. I know now that being rich, is about housing the jewels from the kingdom of heaven: **righteousness, peace** and **joy...** ***(Romans 14:17)*** The value of each of these is priceless. The Lord inspired me to write about these riches, specifically JOY. As you continue to read, you will discover that joy is one of the most valuable, most fulfilling things that you can be.

Joy is one of the key forces in life that will positively enrich any situation in life. Joy enriches life itself.

~The Conception of "Urban Joy" ~

The Lord came into my heart, and my innate sense to care for people heightened. I am drawn to people who are not experiencing the privilege of joy on a daily basis. My compassion to help people who live lives of sadness, are in pain, and are bound to misery, always seem to stir me to pray and give words of encouragement. I give all credit and glory to the Lord, who inspired me to write this book for the purpose of revealing the awesome effect of joy in our everyday living. He also instructed me to entitle the book ***Urban Joy***. Why ***Urban Joy?*** I thought and thought. *"Joy"* I knew, but I did not have a clue of why "*Urban."* I deemed it crucial to get understanding because the life-flow of a book stems from the title. I take to heart ***Proverbs 4:7*** (KJV) which says, "Wisdom is the principal thing; therefore get wisdom: and with all thy getting get understanding." I believe that the light of wisdom coupled with understanding dispels the darkness of ignorance, separates men from boys, transitions good to best and failure to success. I was hoping that all of my efforts of getting understanding would ultimately help people to succeed at being joyful.

In pursuit of getting God's wisdom and understanding of the concept, I decided to do what I knew best and that was to pray and expect God to enlighten me. I also decided to research online the *Free Dictionary by Farlex* for the definition of "urban" even though I thought I knew. Well, it meant exactly what I thought. ***Urban*** is defined as *typical of a city or city life*. After affirming the meaning of the word, I pondered on being raised in the city to see if there was some sort of connection. My thoughts of living in the city did not unveil anything concerning the title being ***Urban Joy***. A bright idea did not illuminate in my mind, I didn't get chill bumps or doo-dads tingling up my spine. I got nothing but a feeling of my thoughts hitting a brick wall and falling flat to the ground. The title of the book remained a mystery until months later. The revelation unfolded while I was home recovering from a hysterectomy that caused me much pain and suffering. I was held together internally by thirty-seven stitches. My activities were limited to reading, praying, listening to CDs and watching television in bed for about seven weeks.

During my time of reading, I felt prompted to read ***Proverbs 10:15*** (KJV) which says, "A rich man's wealth is his strong city." It was enlightening to be able to connect ***Urban*** metaphorically to *strong city.* and a *rich man's wealth* to ***Joy***. I began to dissect the scripture by getting the definitions of the word wealth again from the online *Free Dictionary by Farlex*. The definitions are as follows:

1. ***An abundance of valuable possessions***
2. ***The state of being rich***
3. ***An abundance or profusion of something desirable***

After reading the definitions of wealth, I included joy within the definitions:

1. ***An abundance of joy is one of the most valuable possessions***
2. ***Being joyous is the state of being rich***
3. ***An abundance or profusion of joy is desirable.***

By connecting joy with the definitions of wealth, the analogy unfolded even more. Wealth is likened to joy and the city of a man is likened to a man's heart. "For where your treasure is, there will your heart be also." says Jesus in ***Matthew 6:21*** (KJV). The wealth of joy that a person possesses in their heart is their strong city! If the city of your being is joy, then your whole entire being is joyful. WOW! I have devised a definition for this new phrase.

> ***Urban Joy (ur'ben – joi) 1. Of, relating to, or the characteristic of joy. 2. Being enriched with joy which governs our entire being as a strong city. 3. Joy serving as a magistrate administering its power to flow through the city of a person's heart into the veins of their existence in the midst of pain, suffering, adversity, trials and tribulations.***

When the revelation of ***Urban Joy*** is comprehended, it will be close to impossible to live any other way. Your life will consistently be fortified and strengthened with joy that flows with hope and laughter. ***Urban Joy*** is like being in a strong city that cannot be penetrated. Even though your city may suffer an attack, it will not be seized. ***Urban Joy*** is a type of joy that works like a shield, an immune system and an absolute strength that will enable you to be resilient in maintaining joy even while experiencing harsh realities in life. ***Urban Joy*** will enable you to withstand the storms of life.

A strong city can withstand a category five storm. There may be some damage; however, the entire city is not destroyed. The tragic and historic event of New Orleans being just about completely destroyed happened because the embankment of the city was not strong enough to withstand the forces of Hurricane Katrina. The devastation did not happen because New Orleans did not have the wealth to build up the levees. The levees were neglected and were not fortified sufficiently because of doubt. The city had the wealth to build but those responsible declined using that wealth to make the city strong enough to withstand that type of storm. They doubted that a storm of that severity would come.

In everyone's life, storms come and go. Each of us is responsible for making certain that the city of his or her being is strong enough to withstand the storms of life. Let us not be like those who have chosen to neglect to protect their city. Let us not be like those who doubted that a storm of that severity would come. We can build up our city and protect it with a wealth of joy. This wealth of joy has been provided to keep our city strong and protected. One may attest that they experience joy from time to time. But in all curiosity, one may ask, "Where can this wealth of joy be found?" I have personally found it in close relationship with the multi-facets of our Lord. Many know him as the One who is saving us from eternal damnation, but He is so much more than that. He did not only secure where we will spend eternity ***(John 3:36)***, He is also a very present help in the time of trouble ***(Psalm 46:1)***. We can live a quality life daily because Christ has promised that in Him, our joy can be made **full** ***(St. John 16:24).*** I emphasize the word "**full**" because it depicts being enriched, fortified and built up to the **max**. We need the fullness of joy to help us through the storms of life. We need to know how to tap into that fullness of joy that has been provided.

Many of us profess Christ and strive to one day make it to heaven. But it is evident that many of us do not possess the benefits of knowing Him in our everyday living. Christ has freely given us a wealth of joy to be strong and live a quality life every day. However, in order to possess what He has given, we must accept and understand what has been given. If you are not continuously joyful, you have not completely accepted His offer. As you continue to read, a greater understanding will come and step-by-step you will discover how to accept and acknowledge what has been freely given. You will be empowered and joyfully blessed to exemplify the benefits.

There have been times in my life when someone offered me a gift of some sort and I chose to decline the offer. I would not accept the offer because I was either content with what I had, or not trusting of the giver's motive. Whatever the case may have been, by not accepting the gift, I did not enjoy the benefits of the gift. If you are declining His offer, sincerely give some thought to your reasons why. Maybe you are not aware that you are. Maybe you are overwhelmed with your thoughts, preconceived ideas and methods. As you continue to read, I encourage you to take the time to identify the subtle reasons why you decline the precious wealth of joy that Christ has given and then be empowered to change. Accept every ounce of His gift of joy and watch your life become more than what you could imagine. You will be irrefutably rich. The city of your inner being will be strong. Remember, "A rich man's wealth is his strong city."

We all can learn from the city of New Orleans' tragic event. The lesson is, do not neglect your city by allowing corroding elements of negativity to weaken you. Fortify the levees of your heart with the characteristics of joy. Like New Orleans, your embankment must be strong to withstand storms, mild or severe. Steer away from living by way of your ineffective thoughts and methods. Do not be doubtful that the storms of life will come because without a shadow of a doubt, they will. Do you want to enjoy the life God has given you? Do you want to enjoy your life even while going through harsh realities? If your answer is *Yes*, stay open to identifying those forces that hinder your joy even if the hindrance is you and how you think. Remember to hold onto the fact that joy is valuable and necessary in living a quality life.

Joy is our insurance policy for keeping our life intact.

I have compiled a collection of scriptures, stories, quotes, steps, information and prayers that offers a new outlook concerning the importance of joy. This book is an excellent source that will help fortify the city within us. It will strengthen and prepare us for the inevitable storms of life. We all have or will have a story to tell. Let us rewrite our future story by living ***Urban Joy***.

~ *Joy Is Powerful* ~

Proverbs 10:15 says, "A rich man's wealth is his strong city." A strong city signifies a place of wealth and power. It also signifies that it is not easily seized or penetrated. The Old Testament is full of stories about strong cities that were sought out to be conquered. In our society today, every city's goal is to possess the wealth and strength to avoid a government takeover. As people, we all have a city functioning within us. In our own city, we have things that govern us, be those things good or bad. God's intent for us is that we be governed by joy. ***Urban Joy*** reveals the great news that the wealth of joy that a person possesses in his heart is his strong city. ***Urban Joy*** is the type of joy that empowers the city within us to withstand the forces that come against us.

In order to fully experience the power of joy, you must **BE** joy which is not quite the same as to have joy. ***Urban Joy*** is the type of joy that you are being as opposed to having. It is not like something that you wear or hold, it is something that you are. We always take off what we wear and we put down or let go of what we are holding. ***Urban Joy*** is authentic and *is* from above. It resides in the core of our being. To **BE** this authentic joy is to allow joy to possess the spirit, soul and body**.** Our minds, wills and emotions are consumed with the characteristics of joy, laughter, merriment, light heartedness, sense of humor, cheerfulness, gladness, positivity, gaiety and so on. The characteristics of joy emanate a glow from within as illustrated on the front cover of the book. It becomes part of us like the other parts of our identity. For instance, we are identified by our name, ethnicity, religion, etc. (e.g.) you are:

- Mary
- Irish
- A Christian
- JOY

The revelation of ***Urban Joy*** helped me to clearly see that joy *never* loses its power and *never* depreciates. There are many adversities to tempt me to think that the power of joy depreciates. But, to the contrary, experiencing ***Urban Joy*** isn't like the experience of purchasing a vehicle at full price but as soon as it is driven off the dealership lot, the vehicle depreciates thousands of dollars in that split second. ***Urban Joy*** is from above and cannot be compared to any substance on earth. It *never* lessens in value. Anything less is not authentic joy. It cannot be substituted or impersonated. Over the years we have seen many Elvis impersonators from Los Angeles to Kalamazoo. Everyone knows that the impersonators are not Elvis. We can *never* convincingly pull off impersonating authentic joy. Elvis will only be Elvis, and joy will only be joy.

In my life, there have been many times that I have tried to put on a front, pretending with a fake smile that I am joy. Joy is something we can *never* fake. When we try to fake it, we are only producing something that is phony, dull, stale and sour; something that is not fresh or authentic. When joy is present, it is so powerful that it cannot be contained. Joy is refreshing to those in its presence. Joy is bright and full of life. Joy is quick and powerful. Joy can sweep through a huge auditorium within a millisecond of time carried by the evidence of spontaneous laughter.

God is ever-present and joy is of God. Since joy is of the Lord, it is also ever-present as He is. In the same way, joy is not something that can be stolen as there is nothing on earth or beyond that has the power to steal God. I have heard many preach the message, "Don't let the devil or people steal your joy." God gave me a revelation that opened my eyes to see that joy is too intertwined in us to be stolen. Joy flows through the veins of our existence because of Him. If we do not choose to express joy during times of temptation, we have actually declined being joy. We deem it more important to ignore the power of joy within us and turn away from living out our inherited blessing. We respond based on who we *were* and not who we *are*. Our inherited gift of joy *never* turns into sadness, depression, annoyance or frustration. Each of those negative emotions stands uniquely apart and is distinctly different. We deem it more important to latch hold of those negative emotions. Our joy has not been stolen. We are not a victim of theft. Our lack of expressing joy is self-inflicted. We choose to put on the costume and character of those negative emotions and act them out.

Sadly, many of us who sincerely claim knowing Christ, decline joy constantly. It seems as if joy is not part of our deliverance. There are those of us who speak of being redeemed, yet live a life bound by misery. We fly off the handle, we are mean, we are sorrowful, we speak curse words and words of violence, we are frustrated, we are hardly ever laughing or smiling, we are always murmuring and magnifying what is wrong. We gripe, complain, and roll our eyes about the idiotic/stupid behavior of others most of the time. We exemplify joy only the few times when things are going our way. Some of us, because of pride, pretend to be joyful to cover up our misery. Let us give up pretending. God's wisdom concerning joy coupled with our understanding can help deliver us from choosing to be so miserable. Let us use the power of joy to disrobe the misery that has neatly woven into the fabric of our lives as we function in our home, church, relationships, and/or in our workplaces.

Our statuses in life, degrees, or titles are not who we are; they stand as being what we are. If we can grasp that who we are is a direct reflection of whose we are, we will be resilient in keeping active the power of joy within us. Through Christ, our reflection reveals that we have been put in right standing with God. It is God who made us in the image and likeness of Himself. One of the fruits of God's Spirit is joy. If the Spirit of God is in us then joy is always in us. When joy, the fruit of God's Spirit, is active in us, we are empowered to stand free of being miserable. Let's be passionate about removing the painted smile that serves as a cover-up. Our passion must begin with a commitment to rid ourselves of being bloated with misery.

We all have to take a spiritual enema from time to time to remove the waste of negativity in our lives.

Now if you will, do an exercise with me. This is an exercise that can be practiced often removing the waste of negativity in our lives.

1. **Identify all of your unhappiness. Think about every aspect of your life, even those hidden thoughts of discontent.**
2. **Name the negative emotions that you are holding onto because of your discontent**. (Ex: guilt, feeling sorry for yourself, depressed, irritated, frustrated, resentful, bitter, etc.)
3. **Now see the multi-facets of Christ (**Prince of Peace, Merciful Savior, Wisdom, Friend, Deliverer, Provider, Anointed One who destroys every yoke of bondage that easily beset us**) as being the solution flowing through our entire being removing all of the waste of negativity in us**.
4. **Finally, *Pray*** and ask the Lord to remove the waste of

negativity in your life. Ask God to help you cast down every emotion, thought, imagination that you exalt above the knowledge of Him being in you and part of you.

When you need peace, He will give you peace. When you need forgiveness, He will be merciful and forgive you. When you need to be released from the shackles of things that oppose you, He will deliver you. When you need encouragement, He will be a friend and encourage you. When you just don't know what to do, He will give you guidance and wisdom. When you are mean, hateful, stubborn, bitter and envious because of past offenses and jealousy, He will renew within you a right spirit. Through it all, He will give you His unspeakable joy and a quality of living.

If we want to grasp the revelation of how crucial and beneficial joy is to having a quality life, we must grasp the reality that every day there will be something unfavorable, harsh or not to our liking. In grasping this reality, we must develop a sense of urgency to *always* position ourselves and connect ourselves to the Source (the Lord) and resources that will *always* help us to focus on being influenced by joy. Being influenced by joy absolutely empowers us to respond positively and productively. Joy will not remove the situation but it will enhance and enrich any situation in life.

Misery clouds our minds but joy enlightens it.

Joy will give us the inner strength to break away from the grip of misery. Strength is an attribute of joy as revealed in ***Nehemiah 8:10*** (KJV), "The joy of the Lord is your strength."

If we want the power of joy to govern and strengthen our city within, we must recognize the characteristics of joy in us and around us. Over the years I have discovered that like God, joy is everywhere. Joy is in the form of someone's smile, laughter, encouraging word, hug, kiss, facial expression and or in the many gifted and talented people around us. Some of those gifted people don't even realize that they are natural-born comedians. They are always saying or doing something funny even if they are not trying. It does not matter where they are or what they are doing, they flow naturally in making people laugh. They themselves can be in a funky mood but their gift still stirs up laughter. I have some co-workers who are like that, especially Bradley. I thank

God for them because our job can be stressful and tiring. I am just giggling throughout the day because they consistently say or do something funny, even if they are not trying. I wholeheartedly believe that people like them are a gift to us to keep joy flowing.

It is so beneficial to be able to recognize and appreciate the people and things that keep our joy flowing. We should not stifle the things that encourage our joy's flow. I have seen children do comical things. However, the parents, not recognizing their gift, would shut them down. The childrens' comedic behavior would be labeled as being something else. That child's gift could be used to divert the parents from being frustrated, stressed out and such like. Children are a blessing. God's word says that we are happy when we have them ***(Psalms 127:5)***. I believe that as long as things are done decently and in order, we should encourage those things that keep joy flowing. Just think about it. Why is it automatic for us to brighten up when a baby smiles or giggles? Why? It is because that baby illustrates the characteristic of joy in its purest form. I practice daily to absorb the characteristics of joy around me. This is one way I have learned how to be fully charged by joy. By *being* joy, I believe that I am one of the richest women in the world. However, my currency is joy. I believe that one of my purposes in life is to get as many people to realize how rich they can be by allowing joy to govern them.

The characteristics of joy are like an AC adapter to a laptop computer. Joy is the charge that enables us to boot up the joy within for the challenges ahead. We must recognize the characteristics of joy. We also must recognize our joy adversaries. Recognizing both gives us the capability to quickly identify those things that cause us to decline joy daily, things like being bothered by others' idiotic behavior or thinking on things that are not helpful or beneficial. By being able to recognize both, we are better able to choose one over the other. Owning the revelation of ***Urban Joy***, if joy is behind door number one, door number one will be chosen. The one time out of many that we do not express joy, God gives us 'til morning to get it together. ***Psalms 30:5*** (KJV) says, "Weeping may endure for a night, but joy comes in the morning." God knows that life's circumstances may take us by surprise and may initially be quite difficult for us to adjust to the detriment. Joy comes in the morning when we get a grip on God being all-powerful, all-knowing, always with us and always in control. The moment we grasp who God is in our lives, is the moment our resilience kicks in.

Life can throw some pretty hard punches. Sometimes it could take the wind right out of us and will drop us to our knees. At those times, while we are on our knees, we should pray and purposely look for our Joy AC Adapters. It really helps! Prayer will help us to remain light-hearted because the Lord will lighten our hearts from every trouble. Our Joy AC Adapters will help us to be able to sincerely laugh and smile through the difficulties. There have been times that I would be hit so hard that I would be right at the brink of tears and one of those gifted comedic people would say something funny. Even with the tears escaping my eyes, like water breaking through a levee, I would burst out laughing. Laughter helps us to adjust ourselves to be in the right spirit. The best part of laughter is that it feels really good especially during those tough times. If or when you get hit hard, do not hold back your laughter. Do not resist with a bad attitude and say things like, "Nothing's funny." Always look for your Joy AC Adapters and seize the opportunity to laugh because you will feel so much better.

Pets can also be Joy AC Adapters during those times. The TV hit "Funniest Home Videos" is flooded with people's pets doing some funny things. My sister, Yolanda, could probably be a winner on that show because she has a comical orange and white cat named Creamy. He was abandoned prematurely so my sister nurtured him and now he has grown up to be quite interesting to say the least. He does many funny things. He acts like a dog and at times, human. One of the funniest episodes of this cat is how he uses his litter box. He has a nice-sized litter box in which he can maneuver at will. However, as he squats to handle his business, he chooses to stand upright with his two front paws spread up against the wall like he is being frisked by the police. Get this, being near him is out of the question because he would stop doing his business, and look over his shoulder with this facial expression as if to say, "Do you mind? Privacy Ple-ease!" Time after time, we get a good laugh.

Laughter, being a character of joy, is good for us and has a healing effect like medicine. The *Bible* says in ***Proverbs 17:22*** (KJV), "A merry heart does good like a medicine; but a broken spirit dries the bones." The Bible is a spiritual wonder; it was written thousands of years before doctors discovered how very healthy laughter is for our bodies. Mark Twain, American author and humorist, said, "Against the assault of laughter nothing can stand."

Joy is so powerful that it will evict any dark feeling of emotion.

Joy is the source that helps me escape being broken down, unhappy, depressed, moody, annoyed, frustrated and so on. Many times I escape acting out those negative emotions by recognizing joy in a funny sound, observing how comical a person looks, hearing the humor in something someone says, seeing the animation of something serious or actually seeing how ridiculous and comical a matter is. It is imperative that we recognize and absorb the characteristics of joy every day. Practice over and over to flow with joy. Frustration, stress, sadness, annoyance, depression and so on will lessen and lessen, until one day you will wake up and find yourself living a powerful joyous life continuously.

At this time, take a break from reading, and do an exercise with me. Just take one minute and think of a time when you laughed so long and hard that it was hard to stand and breathe. Tears may have flooded your eyes. Are you thinking? (Pause) Are you reflecting on that moment? (Pause) Do you remember how you felt when you were laughing? (Pause) Now, while you are reflecting, are you smiling? If you are reflecting on a joyous moment, no matter what you are going through right now, you forgot about it. If you are tired, the feeling is gone. If you feel sick, the feeling just left you. If you are frustrated, you're not anymore! Right now you feel good just by reflecting on a joyous moment. Joy is that powerful! It will wipe away any negative emotion.

One of the timeless moments that I reflect upon is something that happened with my dad and me. It brings me joy every time I think about it. At the age of thirty-seven, I had become acquainted with my biological father, and I decided to go visit him one night. I had not seen him in a while. I missed him and could not wait to kiss his cheeks. When I arrived, he was sleeping, so I went to his bedroom with much anticipation to finally see him. I decided to wake him with a kiss. He did not wake up, so I stroked him across his face with my hand and said "Poppy" in a soft tone. As he slooowwwly opened his puffy eyes, to my surprise, he looked at me in a daze as if he did not know me while his body quivered from his toes to his eye balls all within a second. Completely startled, he just stared at me with fright in his eyes. Concerned, I said, "Dad, are you alright?" After a few more stares immobilized in fear, He spoke and said with much expression, "Girl!! Wooooofh!"

Dad went on to explain that he thought I was this seven-foot-tall, bushy-haired woman who he saw in a nightmare one night in his hallway. He explained that in the dream, he prayed in fear that the woman would stay in the hallway and not come in his bedroom. When he saw me towering over him (my hair was big and puffy that night), he thought I was her coming back to haunt him again, but this time, at his bedside. As he continued to tell me about his experience, I could no longer stand from laughing so hard. I hit the floor. Everything I saw was blurred because of my tears of joy. I think I was on the floor a good ten minutes trying to get up. But each time I would get up, I went back down laughing all over again. It hurt so good as my stomach muscles tightened. I was laughing so much that once my dad gathered himself, he started to laugh heartily as well. **Joy is contagious.** Reflect on the times when you got a good laugh. It's good for the soul. Family and friend gatherings are a perfect time to reflect on the comical things shared together over the years. Those comedic moments house a substance that strengthens the roots of relationships. Before family and friend gatherings, **Pray** that God will bless your coming together with good memories. Ask God to let His love and joy flow from heart to heart. From my experience, this prayer works. As our gathering comes to an end, we always leave laughing and feeling good. Many times when we end being together, I sing the Carol Burnett song of benediction. I let everyone know in song how glad I was that we had our time together. I mention our laughing and maybe singing together. Good times are never long enough because it seems that just when we get started, we wind up having to say goodbye.

I would like to sum up this chapter by saying joy is so powerful that it will remove the waste of negativity in us. It will evict every negative emotion. It is worth the effort to connect ourselves with the Source (the Lord) and resources that will help us focus on being empowered. It is worth the effort of taking advantage of the Joy AC Adapters around us. It is worth seeing the humor in something. It is worth hugging, kissing, smiling, laughing, enjoying a baby's giggle, and etc. Life is too short not to enjoy it every day. Who knows when our number will come up? It could be today, next week, next year. . . . Every day the power of joy can usher us out of living the 3M's:

Mediocrity
Mess
Misery

to living the 3E's:

Extraordinary
Elated
Exceptional

Urban Joy is God's divine magistrate that enforces His spiritual laws in the inner city of our being to empower and govern us to be happy.

~ *A Gift from Above* ~

Joy is most definitely a gift from above. I see joy as a priceless, unbiased, and a multicultural gift from God. It is refreshing, positive, and enhances everything it touches. This priceless gift cannot be produced by a drug, manufactured, cloned or ingeniously created through technology. God has created us in His image and likeness. Operating in our divine ability to create and invent, we have created some superficial methods of joy to escape some of the harsh realities in life. For instance, MSN reported a new mood drug designed to make people happy. The report stated that the drug's effect would cause people to think happy thoughts. It is a costly drug that requires a prescription. To get a temporary feeling of ecstasy, some people have been known to lick poison off the backs of toads. In another instance, it has been discovered that eating (psilocybin) mushrooms causes a heightened happy effect. I have had conversations with some who reported that after eating the mushrooms, they laughed for seven to eight hours straight without moving from the same spot. The irony of this discovery is that the high effect is stimulated from the dried manure coated on the mushrooms. Authentic joy is pure. You do not have to eat poo to laugh continually. You do not have to lick poison to feel good. You do not have to be dependent on a costly drug to help you think happy thoughts. The everlasting gift of joy that is from above is free, foolproof . . . and it has no bad side effects

There is a simple contingency in receiving this free gift of joy. All we need to do is open up our minds and hearts to receive. Before I got the revelation of the value of joy, my heart and mind were not opened because I had misconceptions about joy.

The prophets trained by Christian International Ministry prophesied, "God has gifted you with joy." They said, "God called you a woman of joy, a woman that will inject joy, and a woman that will bring joy to the Body of Christ." Early in my Christian walk, everyone that gave me prophetic words mentioned something about joy. I really did not appreciate those words. I would always want to hear something else. I did not think that a woman of joy held much significance. I knew that it was nice to be a joyful person, but in my mind, I thought, "Who would take seriously a person that walked around with a smile on her face all of the time?" I wanted people to look at me like I was a serious, powerful, black woman. I imagined being so powerful that the song *I've Got the* Power (as recorded by C+C Music Factory) would play as my background music when I walked into a room. I'm just kidding. Okay, not really. . . the thought has occurred to me quite a few times.

If I could put words to my attitude about constantly having joy pronounced over me, it would be "All right, already, I know that I am called to be, give, and inject joy. Let's not run it down to the ground. Isn't there something else you want to say to me, Lord?" It was so wrong for me to have that attitude. I imagined that God said, "Oh, you want to have that attitude? You say you want to hear something else? I can fix that. I'll give you something else to hear."

Around that time when I had that awful attitude concerning being a woman of joy, I was attending a "Prophetic Activation" church service (a format in which a team of people are selected to activate and practice their prophetic gifts by giving a word from God to a person who is randomly selected from the congregation). I was selected! I felt soooo special. I was excited because the people who were chosen before me were getting good words like "God is calling you to the nations; God is going to use you mightily, and God is going to give you wealth." That was the stuff I was hoping to hear.

When it was my turn, seven out of the eight people came up to me and prophesied short word phrases like this, "Joy, joy, joy, woman of joy, I see joy, and or joy lady." They ran with that joy thing so much that I could have stuck my finger down my throat. I thought, "God is not telling them that! Goodness gracious, these church folk act like dumb sheep. They are only saying things about joy because they heard others pronounce that over me. Why can't they be original, stop making stuff up and tell me what God is really saying?" With me having that bad attitude, I believe that the following account happened for me to learn a lesson.

The eighth person was a woman who was fairly new to the church. I was hoping that she had not been influenced by the others. She got the microphone and walked up to me and spoke slowly, so much so that it seemed like time stopped and everyone stopped breathing for a moment. She said it with a nicotine-invaded, deep raspy voice, "I hear, I hear, 'Clean that man's house!'" Then she had the nerve to say in a puzzled tone, "That's all I hear." When she stopped speaking, some of the congregation laughed so hard that they were red in the face. Tears rolled down their cheeks, especially my cousin Trisha. With my borderline OCD behavior, I was appalled that she gave that word. I felt defensive and wanted to say something, but I knew it would not be appropriate. So I thought, "My house is clean. *Thank you very much!* Anyone that knows me knows that my house is clean."

Then my thoughts were directed towards her, "Maybe that is a personal word from God for *you*, Missy!" I thought that thought with every ghetto bone in my body. I imagined saying it with two quick snaps of my fingers being snapped in her face. I eventually realized that there was no need for me to have that self-righteous ghetto attitude. The moral of this lesson is that I should have received the Word of the Lord about joy with joy. Isn't that ironic? The joke was on me. Who said that God does not have a sense of humor? I would also like to interject, be careful about what you ask for and be appreciative of what you have.

I should have allowed my heart and mind to be opened to this precious gift. In retrospect, I was very immature. I really did not see the significance of envisioning myself as a woman of joy. I thank God that the revelation came. However, it did not come without a price, the price of blood, sweat and tears. I am a living witness that this precious gift that God has given me has been majorly tested, tried, and proven to be authentic. In paying the price, my thinking changed. I have a new perspective on life. I had to change my mindset and open my eyes to the reality of the necessity of joy on a daily basis. Do you envision yourself as a man or woman of joy? If not, **Pray** and ask God to help you to identify the reasons why and the challenges associated with the reasons. Ask Him to give you the strength and courage to change in those areas.

I had to change my belief that being joyous equated to not being powerful. I thought that a joyous person was a cream puff, and who would listen to a cream puff? I had to stop thinking that people of joy are not in touch with reality, that they cannot set matters straight. I even thought that God only used mightily the people who had "power gifts" (Working of Miracles, Gift of Faith, Gift of Healing). Oh, was I wrong!

The Lord has shown me that being a joyful person operates like a power gift. The power of joy will bring anyone out of the grips of depression. I have seen people snatched away from the clutches of suicidal thoughts because of my joy. My joy has effectively made a significant change in many lives. They are happier. They no longer accept gloom and misery to be normal. I have seen them put up a fight. They have become junkies for joy. Even when people are angry with me, I have seen my joy turn that frown upside down. We can be joy and we can make a difference in so many people's lives.

One prophet said to me, "God has smeared you with His joy that will bring healing to people emotionally and physically." This word has come to pass on numerous occasions. Countless times people were brought out of a state of being deeply hurt by way of something as simple as my smile, laughter, singing, making a gesture or saying something funny. When people around me are feeling drab, dull, down, or bored, I have seen my joy break the monotony and cause an entire room of people to laugh and have a good time. There have been times when my joy has sparked laughter within individuals whose bodies were wracked with pain. Those individuals have testified to me that after laughing, they no longer felt their pain. Just imagine if every member of the medical field housed joy . . . what a difference that would make for so many people. I am sure a lot fewer prescriptions would be written as well. Just imagine if all bosses, managers, supervisors and employees housed joy, it would make for a productive atmosphere. Just imagine if every wife and husband housed joy, what a difference it would make in raising children and keeping the family intact.

Being joy is a powerful and infectious gift. I have an assignment for you. Make this observation when you are being joyous. Walk into a room full of gloom and observe the faces in the room brighten up just because of your presence. Laugh and watch people who were not compelled to laugh start laughing. I can personally testify that people will miss your presence when you are absent. The Lord has called me to be joy and to help others to get the revelation of being joy. I am devoted daily to continue this quest until I reach heaven. I see the importance to strive to be Joy. The dark, harsh realities of life will continue until our journey in this world ends.

God has given us His gift of joy as a warm ray of sunshine to dispel the dark, cold realities that we will undoubtedly face.

~ *Joy Now!* ~

Being ***Urban Joy*** is being *Joy Now*! ***Urban Joy*** is authentic joy that is always present tense. It is not based on the joy we had in the past. It is not based on the joy we may see in the future. It is a present state that we choose to be right now, no matter what is going on in our lives.

The present state of joy, that we choose to be, aids us in having a very fierce attitude in the right direction.

The online *Free Dictionary by Farlex* defines *Attitude* as *"A settled way of thinking or feeling, typically reflected in a person's behavior; it is a position of the body, or manner of carrying oneself.*" ***Urban Joy*** is an attitude of intensity that will set our mind to stay positive. With all that we go through in life, we need to be able to tap into a source that will fortify us to be staunched in living a joyful life.

I have found that because of the harsh realities that we face and/or see daily, we need to bypass the ineffective, mediocre, humanistic level of joy. We must tap into a greater source of joy in order to maintain our stance. Intimately knowing Christ is what gives us this great joy***. Luke 2:10*** reveals to know Jesus, "Great joy is for all." Intimately knowing Christ goes far beyond attending church, wearing a WWJD bracelet, and driving around with the fish mounted on the backs of our vehicles for all to see. Knowing Christ is actually developing a very personal close relationship with Him. Developing a very close relationship with an influential, powerful friend is the same as getting to know Christ. For instance, we learn their ways, we cherish their opinions and we actually start emulating them. When we start emulating our Lord, we are empowered with great joy. That is God's promise to us.

As Christians, we are so privileged. It is our inheritance to be *Joy* always in the *Now!* We can take advantage of our inheritance regardless of what happens. Christ knew that His rightful place was to sit on the right hand of God after He reconciled us back to the Father. Christ did not let anything stop Him from doing what it took to get there. Like Christ, we should know our inheritance and we should not let anything stop us from being joy. **Pray** and ask God for the tenacity to express your inherited joy in every situation. What matters most is not what has happened to us, it is how we respond to what has happened. We can take control of the reigns of our lives. We have the power to adjust the reigns to steer away from our negative emotions. A joyful, positive attitude is what empowers us to successfully control our emotions. Many of us live our lives without even thinking about joy. We just live and react to what may come. It is as if we live our lives on a roller coaster of emotions, we are up and down and all around. We are unstable. Emulating our Lord and taking advantage of our inheritance empowers us to behave differently. Being empowered by joy is like experiencing stability on steroids.

On the other hand, I have noticed some twisted behaviors while interacting with people. Their joy is of a different nature. I have noticed that some delight in acting ugly -- and it appears that they are even proud of it. They get a joy out of instigating, antagonizing and stirring up messes. These people have what I call "The Tales from the Crypt" type of joy. Like the people in that TV horror show, they also get a delight out of being mean, selfish and uncaring. They get some kind of freakish happiness and satisfaction from being negative and sarcastic. They take pride in their skillful ability to insult someone. I have noticed that these types of people have a tendency to say, "I'm just kidding or just ignore me!" after they have hit you with their negativity. They expect you to laugh or be happy about their negativity. Frequently they have haughty, uncaring attitudes about the feelings of others and in some eerie way, they think that their "Dark Side" behavior is good. I say that type of behavior is only good if Darth Vader *"isss yooour faaatherrr."*

If you are wondering where you presently fit in all of this, take the Behavior Diagnostic Test. Involve the people closest to you. Ask them to rate you by putting a check under the characteristics that best describe your behavior. Once you are rated, please do not get defensive, argue and or fight, because if you do, you will only affirm their answers. If you are given the privilege to rate, please be courageously and tactfully honest. People need to know the truth to distinctively and effectively change. ***John 8:32*** (KJV)***:*** "And ye shall know the truth, and the truth shall make you free."

We all need to face the truth about our ways that need to change in order for us to freely live a more quality joyful life.

Behavior Diagnostic Test

	All of the time	*Most of the time*	*Sometimes*	*Never*
***Moody**	______	______	______	______
***Frustrated**	______	______	______	______
***Depressing**	______	______	______	______
***Negative**	______	______	______	______
Positive	______	______	______	______
***Uptight**	______	______	______	______
***Sarcastic**	______	______	______	______
***Mean/difficult**	______	______	______	______
Optimistic	______	______	______	______
***Pessimistic**	______	______	______	______
Light Hearted	______	______	______	______
Laugh	______	______	______	______
***Short Tempered**	______	______	______	______
***Angry**	______	______	______	______
Joyful	______	______	______	______

*Characteristics that corrode living a quality joyful life.

* * *

Once you have been rated by a few closest to you, please do not spiritualize or justify your negative behavior, especially if you hold a leadership position. We must stop the insanity of thinking that we are going to have a stable, healthy, joyful environment in our workplace, home, church or anywhere, if we consistently behave negatively.

"Insanity is doing the same thing over and over again expecting a different result." -- Albert Einstein

We must lead by example. We set the momentum in our surroundings. In order to lead by example, we must have a broken and contrite spirit. Being broken, we rest in an humble state. We are void of pride, haughtiness, impatience and meanness. Having a contrite spirit, we are free of bitterness, strife, resentment and jealousies. When your heart is free of these things, you will not gravitate to being negative. You will be the bliss (joy) of heaven. Your interactions with others will be an illumination of God's glory. People will respect you, appreciate you, appreciate your words, follow you, trust you, and enjoy being around you.

Throughout my life in Christ, I have noticed that when it comes to being joy, we repeatedly make excuses for why we are not. Many times, we feel like we have a right to act ugly. Many of us like to walk in an *"it's a process"* mentality. This mentality supports the justification of wasting dear time getting around to being joy. There seems to be a sense of pride and obligation to go through negative moods or emotions while experiencing trials. This is done because of what is ingrained in our patterns of thinking. Learned behavior conditions us to mimic what we see. Many of us may not verbalize this, but we demonstrate a haughty attitude by thinking in our mind, "I have a right to behave this way because I am human." A soldier is trained to think beyond the attitude of being human. His focus is to protect at any cost. We should take on the attitude of a soldier. Our precious joy is worth protecting. Walking in the "*it's a process*" mentality does not house the attitude of a soldier. That type mentality justifies declining joy and acting like a fool at times.

The TV comedy "Martin" that aired some years back, depicted this type of behavior exaggerated to the tenth power. In a particular scene, one of the female characters was acting distraught in church. She was expressing her negative emotions by hollering and screaming, flipping down the aisle, and biting the wood off of the pews. I found that scene to be particularly funny. I could relate to it, having seen people attend family funerals who did similar things. They hollered, screamed, and called out the deceased name as if the deceased was going to lift his or her head up and answer by saying, "Yeeeess?" These same people would also collapse and the men, like pallbearers, would hold them up and carry them to their seats. Their bodies would be so limp that their feet would drag on the carpet. These same distraught people would later regain strength and attempt to climb into the casket. These performances were something to see . . . and were done without a script.

Many of us do not realize that to be grievous, moody, sad, frustrated, and or mad, is just as easy as being *Joy Now!* It is just as easy because our emotions are fortified by our thoughts. If we are consumed with grievous thoughts, we will grieve. If we dwell on things that are frustrating, we will be frustrated. If we think on things that are joyous, we will be joy. Our thoughts that we allow to settle in our minds like sediment are what we will become. As you journey through life, comply with practices that are in your favor and based on the probability of a positive outcome. In reading, I have discovered that a well-determined group of masterminds form think tanks to use mathematics and physics to equate the most appropriate solution to the major economic, military, energy, and infrastructure challenges that face mankind? I am no mastermind, but I have formulated an equation that serves as a mnemonic device called the "Think Tank Equation." It can be implemented in the privacy of our home, in the car, at work and virtually where ever we are to intelligently equate the outcome of thoughts while dealing with the challenges we face.

"Think Tank Equation"

Proverbs 23:7

"For as he thinketh in his heart, so is he: ……." (KJV)

"As he calculates the cost to himself, this is what he does" (NOGBV)

Grievous thoughts = Being grievous
Frustrating thoughts = Being frustrated
Jealous thoughts = Being jealous
Loving thoughts = Being loving
Joyous thoughts = Being joyous
Happy thoughts = Being happy

Doctors have discovered the capabilities in how our mind and brain has been created to function. Dr. Siegel, an author of several books, professor of psychiatry at UCLA school of Medicine, co-director of the UCLA Mindfulness Awareness Research Center, Executive Director of the Mindsight Institute, has created the term "mindsight." Dr. Siegel describe *mindsight* as being the human capacity to perceive the mind of the self and others. On his website, Siegel writes, *Mindsight is a kind of focused attention that allows us to see the internal workings of our own minds. It helps us get ourselves off of the autopilot of ingrained behavior and habitual responses. It lets us "name and tame" the emotions we are experiencing, rather than being overwhelmed by them.*

Much time and effort has gone into researching our cognitive functioning. Scientists like Dr. Siegel have tapped into how our Omniscient God has created our minds to function. ***Philippians 4:8*** speaks directly to our potential to "tame" the emotions we experience by thinking on the right things. It says, "Finally, brothers and sisters, whatever is true, whatever is noble, whatever is right, whatever is pure, whatever is lovely, whatever is admirable; If anything be excellent or praiseworthy, think on these things." We can think on these things even when we have to resolve conflict, troubleshoot, transact business, or deal with pain, disappointment and tragedy. We are capable of being well-rounded in looking for solutions and good results rather than being overwhelmed by negative emotions.

When my daughters were young, I would make them put smiles on their faces when I saw that they had bad attitudes about their little trials or being corrected. Instead of sending them to their room to sulk in misery, I wanted to instill in them the ability to be *Joy Now!* in spite of their circumstances. I wanted them to see beyond how things appeared. I also wanted them to be able to remain stable even though things were not going their way. They can attest that it is very hard to think on negative things with big smiles on their faces. Many times I would stir up their laughter by laughing at how funny their faces looked when they attempted to smile. They would start out with some resistance by dropping their jaws and protruding their bottom teeth, while their little eyes revealed the opposite. Their faces would look so funny. My laughter would trigger us laughing together.

I wanted them to see that their whole day didn't have to be ruined because they had a little trial. I would not let them justify being negative. When they saw that I would not waiver, would reroute their thinking and they would be back to laughing and playing in a short period of time. They are grown now and are living a resilient life because of their training. I thank God! We have gone through much as a family, however, we still have a bond to help each other to stay on course of being joy. We have so much fun when we get together. Frequently we call each other, Skype or text with funny stories that keep our joy flowing and our family bonded. We keep each other in check. We help each other steer away from the negative thinking that stirs negative emotions.

In my book, there are two legitimate reasons why people can't steer away from negative thinking, (1) neural malfunctions and or (2) demonic possession. In these two cases, major medical attention or an exorcism is needed. However, if you are not mentally malfunctioning or possessed, you should thank God that you are capable of being *Joy Now!* My customer James wanted to desperately trade out of his new car that he really liked and worked so hard to get. He explained that he was taking his childhood friend to get medical attention. His friend, being tormented, took a suicidal leap out of his vehicle while moving at an accelerated pace. He was only a matter of minutes away of getting the help that he needed. If we are capable of steering away from negative emotions in our present state of being, then we should realize how fortunate we are. We should count our blessings, and be *Joy Now!*

I have counseled many and tried to help them see that joy is a key factor needed while they were going through rough patches in their lives. Some would perceive "being joy" as not having a grip on reality. I have heard counless times, "You just don't understand," or, "That's easy for you to say." Those who said such things felt their situations warranted them *not* to be joy. Before I got the revelation of ***Urban Joy,*** I have even said those things myself when someone would try and get me out of a funk. I said those things because I wanted to dwell more on what was bringing me sorrow. Wallowing more into what I was going through fed my misery. Truthfully, understanding what you are going through is not what is important. What's important weighs heavily on how you are going to get through it successfully. Our joy is a key component in being successful.

If we can really grasp the understanding that God created us to be able to change our mind, we can successfully reroute our emotions. It is a daily practice of mine to reroute my thinking and then ultimately my emotions. ***Ephesians 4:23*** (KJV) says, "And be renewed in the spirit of your mind." In the course of changing my mind, I have learned to change my body position as well. I remove myself from the fog of my troubles and focus on what I am doing, when I am doing it, and how I am doing it. For instance, the process of rerouting my thoughts include all of the following:

- I deliberately pull away from thinking about what is bringing me trouble.
- I emotionally leave what I cannot handle with God in prayer.
- I seize any and every opportunity to laugh. I look for my Joy AC Adapters.
- I go out with friends and or family and have a good time.
- I get involved in helping others.
- I get involved with a constructive project.
- I go to church, enjoy praise and worship, and enjoy hearing the Word of God.
- I read and meditate on specific scriptures that directly address what I am going through.
- I sing.
- I read this book, ***Urban Joy***, over and over again.

I am hoping to help many to see that joy is not some unrealistic silly state of being. Joy is a state of being that is real, obtainable and seriously light- hearted which helps us remain positive during current adversities. Let's make it our business to obligate ourselves to be no other way but *Joy Now!* Whatever you put your heart and mind to do, you will do it. Do not ever think that being joy now means you have to do it alone. Remember ***Philippians 4:13*** (KJV) says, "I can do all things through Christ who strengthens me." It is because of Christ that we can presently be filled with great joy. We do not have to settle for excuses. Our cognitive faculties help us to understand our inner states of being, and with the help of the Lord, we can steer away from negative thinking. God has created us with the capability to be *Joy Now!* To quote the Nike, slogan: *Just Do It.* When we *just do it* we will always experience in the present the beauty of joyful living.

~ *Fruit of the Spirit* ~

Galatians 5:22-23 (KJV) says, "The fruit of the Spirit is love, **joy**, peace, longsuffering, gentleness, goodness, faith, meekness, temperance; against such there is no law." As you can see, the *Bible* describes joy as being one the fruit of the Spirit of God. This explains why joy is so powerful and effective to the human race. It is a characteristic that sets us apart from any other species. Unlike other species, we understand cause and effect and socialize with each other in meaningful ways. When we socialize with each other, we find ourselves laughing, joking and being merry at any given time for many different reasons. We celebrate holidays and birthdays. We have a blast at football tailgate parties. We go to social events, comedy shows, plays, movies, etc. for pleasure. However, I have discovered that there is a difference between the joy of the Spirit of God and delight that is associated with leisure pleasures, social events, addictions, jesting, and making the brunt of the joke to be people's flaws, handicaps and weaknesses.

Comedians make their living by talking about people's flaws, handicaps and weaknesses. They also help us to see the humor in serious matters. They know how to turn a sad situation into hilarity. I enjoy comedies and going to see stand-up comedians that are rated PG. My favorite comedian is Sinbad because his jokes are not vulgar and permeated with profanity. He is like a comedic theologian. His words are zany and truthful. At one of his shows I attended, he gave advice to parents who are having a hard time getting their grown kids to leave the house. He told them to start walking around the house *naked.* He then said if that did not work, to "make love all over the house and begin on the dining room table." He promised that the children would walk out the door, calling the parents "a bunch of nasty's." I could not sit up straight when he said that. Continuously Sinbad had my daughter, her husband and me laughing until we felt our muscles straining.

This type of joy is humanistic, and it can brighten anyone's day. However, the joy from being filled with the Spirit of God is different. The difference is that the core of our being is penetrated supernaturally, ignited by the Spirit of God. The fruit of the Spirit, **joy** goes beyond the humanistic expression of joy. To know the difference is to experience the difference. To experience the difference, you must be filled with the spirit of God. You do not have to be entertained by an outside source to house this type of joy. Being filled with the Spirit of God is as simple as opening your mouth to be filled with good food. You simply open your heart to be filled with the presence of God. When you welcome His presence, you will be quickened (made alive) to live by His word. You will become part of Him as He is part of you. With our core being ignited, God leads us who belong to Him. "For as many as are led by the Spirit of God are the sons of God." ***(Romans 8:14)*** (KJV) Being led by the Spirit of God, we will be led to being joyful. The joy of God's Spirit is pure and will put a glow on our faces and glisten in our eyes. We will be "deep-down-to-the-core" happy regardless of circumstance.

According to *Webster's II New Riverside University Dictionary*, the definitions of *happy* are: 1. Having, displaying, or marked by pleasure or joy; fitting: appropriate; 2. Pleased and **willing**; unduly enthusiastic. Quite naturally, mankind has moments of experiencing happiness in life without the Holy Spirit. Just reflect back on a bar or club scene. People would be drunk silly and having a blast. However, without the Holy Spirit, when things were not so pleasant -- challenging or downright unfortunate -- we have seen people change their expression of joy quicker than bacteria growing on a person's behind that hadn't been washed for days in the summertime. Without the Holy Spirit, people cannot cope with their problems. They are overwhelmed with bad feelings of emotions. Some try to escape by getting high and or getting intoxicated. Some are prescribed all sorts of medications, admitted into mental institutions. Some emotionally go into caves of isolation and depression. Some, unfortunately, commit suicide.

Having God's Holy Spirit in us will take us beyond a humanistic expression of joy. The joy of the Lord is not natural, it is supernatural. We need something supernatural to help us through the overwhelming, unfortunate, often harsh realities of life. Just watch or listen to the news, we see hardship, disaster, tragedy and death everywhere. No one is exempt. The entire human race is affected. According to the *Bible*, in the Book of Genesis, we can give thanks to our forefather Adam, who started the curse of life. We can also give thanks to our Lord and Savior who is the ultimate substitute redeeming us from the curse. Our joy can be made full in this harsh world because of Him.

Joy is defined in the *Webster's II New Riverside University*

Dictionary as *great happiness; delight; a source of happiness undoubted.* The meaning and effects of joy are wonderful. I do not know anyone who does not want to live a life full of its wonder. But why does it seem so hard to be resilient in being joyful? The answer is that we haven't yet tapped into a joy that does not waiver. We are not filled with God's Spirit, which enables us to walk in the Spirit. Walking in the Spirit of God helps us to avoid fulfilling the lust of our flesh ***(Galatians 5:16).*** It is our flesh (natural inclinations) that compels us to be depressed, mad, oppressed, sad, mean, irritable, frustrated, offended, anxious, annoyed and grievous. The works of the flesh can cause so much havoc. However, being joy does not. There is no law, natural or spiritual, against us being joyful in society, in our work place or in our home. Things always tend to run smoothly when we behave in the characteristics of the Spirit of God. In order to allow joy to govern our entire being, we need reinforcements.

Walking in the Spirit and being around like-minded people also helps enforce being governed by joy. If the people we choose to be around a good portion of our time are miserable, depressed, hateful, complainers, and always involved in drama, we will be just like them. Those types of people should be in our outer circle of influence because that type behavior is not something that we should feed on every day. In order to always be a help to them, we need to be influenced and fortified by people of joy. "Birds of a feather flock together." You will never see doves hanging with buzzards. Doves flock with doves; buzzards flock with buzzards. You will never see a dove eat what a buzzard eats. The appetite of a dove is entirely different than that of a buzzard. When you see a buzzard, you know that there is something dead nearby. Buzzards live to eat rotten, stinking, decaying flesh.

A dear friend of mine, Mary Campbell, had a mother who lived to be ninety-eight years of age. We called her Mom Maggie. If Mom Maggie got a notion that a person was doing something wrong, she would directly call the person out and say, "You ol' Buzzard." I was always amazed that this tiny woman would courageously call the "buzzards" out. I always got a good chuckle out of Mom Maggie expressing herself because she did it with attitude. In her expression, her lips would be drawn downward like she smelled a stinking odor. The truth is, the effects of being negative can be compared to something that stinks. Mom Maggie has gone home to be with the Lord, but she has left a memorable joyous impression with me that will live on. Unlike Mom Maggie, we cannot call people out and be as successful as she was at getting away with it. However, we can assess the type of people we are close to in relationship and make the necessary changes. Remembering to treat people the way that we want to be treated will enable us to make a smooth transition of shifting relationships without hurting or abandoning people.

What makes it difficult for many to walk in the Spirit of God is the fact that many do not know much about Him. Many people have some knowledge of Christ. However, they are not too familiar with the Holy Spirit, the fruit of the Holy Spirit or the promises of the Holy Spirit ***(St. John 16:7-15).*** In these scripture verses, Christ promised us that when He returned to heaven, the Holy Spirit would come as (1) the Comforter and (2) the Spirit of Truth. The Comforter's job is to bring us peace, relief, rest, sufficiency, warmth and well-being during the times of trials, tribulation, adversity and hardship. The job of the Spirit of Truth is to guide us and lead us into all truth. There are so many doctrines. We live in a world where the father of lies runs rampant. ***1 Peter 5:8*** speaks of him walking about seeking whoever he can devour. ***Revelation 12:9*** reveals that the devil's aka Satan's main objective is to deceive the whole world. The Spirit of truth is here to protect us from deception and lies. The Spirit of truth will help us to not decline joy and will guide us away from believing lies that will easily set us back.

Many personally live a defeated life because of a lie. Tragically many of us never reach our highest potential because of believing lies. I can personally testify to being trapped into believing a lie about myself. Instead of my thoughts being consumed with my divine purpose, I would constantly be bombarded with thoughts and feelings of negativity. I lived for thirty-six years believing that I was ugly because of bad childhood experiences. No matter how often people told me that I was pretty or attractive, I could not see it. Living in a world of vanity, I was tormented. I declined to be happy with myself because of that ugly lie. The Holy Spirit led me to put two scriptures on my mirror that read, "I am fearfully and wonderfully made" ***Psalm 139:14*** (KJV*),* and "I am beautified with salvation." ***Psalm 149:4*** (KJV) Whenever I would look in the mirror and hear, "You are so ugly," I would replace the lie by saying the scriptures out loud over and over. I did this repeatedly until I realized one day I no longer heard, "You are so ugly." Instead, I heard, "Hey beautiful!" I have lived for several years now believing and knowing that I am beautiful, yet void of conceit. I feel beautiful inside and out.

If you are not happy with yourself, try meditating on those scriptures. From personal experience I can tell you with all sincerity that you will be set free. Now that the lie has been replaced with the truth, I am able to appreciate who I am and how I am created. I stopped comparing myself to others, which only left me with a false, empty feeling of being less or inferior. I am now able to see clearly my own unique beauty. I see myself as God sees me. I no longer see myself through the lies of the airbrushed magazines or the special effects of Hollywood. I no longer starve myself to try to look like a runway model. I am God's model. I can clearly see the things that compliment me, and I stick to what works. I am attentive to the colors that compliment my complexion. I only purchase cuts and designs that compliment my shape. I wear my make-up in a way that compliments my eyes and facial structure. I wear my hair in a way that is becoming. I also work out. There is not one day that goes by that I do not get a compliment. I am humbled because I know why I am getting these compliments: the Spirit of Truth freed me from being trapped into believing a lie. I no longer decline the joy of being happy with myself.

The spirit of truth will extinguish the lies that bring about all feelings of worthlessness. People may be cruel, hateful and belittling; we may not accomplish our goals in life; our children grow up and no longer need us; we are no longer top dog at work; getting up there in age; our beauty and youthful strength fades as things dry up, fall out and wrinkle, all of these occurrences can bring about feelings of worthlessness. The Spirit of Truth will help us to see that our worth is not in what people say or do, it is not in our age, nor in what we have accomplished. Our worth is in to whom we belong. Our worth is in direct connection to our ageless divine purpose. Our worth is defined by a loving, caring, forgiving God who loves us so much that He sent His son to pardon all of the messed up things we have done. He has adopted us where we can boldly go to his throne and call Him Father ***(Romans 8:15).*** We are heirs to His kingdom ***(James 2:5).*** We are royalty which is a far cry from being worthless. ***(1 Peter 2:9)***

Not only will the Holy Spirit help us with our identity, He will give us a vision of hope. If we have lost everything, He will comfort us beyond understanding. The Comforter will also eject the empty dark feeling of loneliness. He will guide us to connect with God and people in heartfelt ways. Meaningful relationships will be formed and will thrive, such that loneliness will not stand a chance. I experienced my marriage being broken and the empty-nest syndrome around the same time. I had never been alone in my entire life. My babies were now grown and living out all that they were trained and nurtured to do, and I was no longer in relationship with my spouse after almost three decades. I experienced the brunt of why God said, "It is not good that man should be alone." ***Genesis 2:18*** (KJV) Loneliness is an awful feeling.

I had begun to go sideways by accepting people in my life that did not have my best interest. I did it just to appease that awful feeling of loneliness. When I saw that being in relationships with those people was subtly pulling me away from God, I stepped back and took a hard look at where I was heading. In the midst of judging myself, the Comforter delivered me from loneliness by helping me to not depend on people to fill any void in my life and simultaneously showed me how to be happy within myself. He brought me to a place that the silence in my home was no longer cold and empty; it is like an ongoing harmonious wave of peace. I am content not having the television playing or having someone there to talk to. However, when I do want to talk to someone or have fellowship, He has given me terrific family members and friends to commune with. I can call my sister Yolanda any time of the night, and she will talk with me without complaint.

The Spirit of Truth will also make it evident that we are loved, as well as, precious ***(Psalms 139:17)*** no matter *who* we have done, *what* we have done, or *how* we have done. He will give us a sense of value and self-worth. The Spirit of Truth is ever present to lead us through the narrow road away from addictions and compromise. The addictions could be induced by food, drugs, alcohol, sex, pornography or other devices that gratify our dysfunctional cravings. I concur with psychologists who say that people fall prey to those things because of the abnormal or impaired functioning in their lives. The dysfunctions causes empty holes in our souls, holes which we all have a sense to want to fill. However, in an attempt to satisfy ourselves, many of us depend upon harmful addictions. All forms of addiction produce pleasure, regardless of how short-lived the effects. They provide an illusion that the gaping hole in one's soul is being filled. However, the attempts to fill our emptiness have proven to be futile and defile us from within. ***(Mathew 15:19-20)*** The spirit of God can repair any abnormal or impaired functioning, ultimately filling the void. That gaping hole in my soul dictated that to be whole I needed people to fill it. I am now in a wonderful place in my life that I am complete and whole within myself. I now function wholly in all relationships but most importantly I do it while staying on course with my divine purpose.

The Holy Spirit is present to guide us into truth, fulfilling any void that we might be experiencing. He will guide us to connect with the right information and special people as well as to guide us to participate in things that will put us in right standing with God. He will bring us to the realization that God is merciful and loves us in spite of our trespasses. He will grace us with the vision of our divine purpose for living, and will guide us into fulfilling our destiny. The Holy Spirit strategically empowers us with knowledge and grace to avoid those depleting dysfunctions in life.

How can one get to a place where the Spirit of God can actively do these things for us? *Right where you are* is the answer! God requires no strain of effort from us. He has done it all. *Right where you are*, just believe and have expectation. *Right where you are,* surrender your mind, will and emotions over to Him. It is a simple act of being receptive and attentive to His guidance. God's Spirit will ignite your spirit. The fruit of being filled with the Spirit of God is the evidence of being free from the strongholds of lies, being void of feeling worthless, being delivered from addictions and dysfunctions, being released from the shackles of loneliness, depression . . . and so much more.

The fruit of God's Spirit is why we can experience that deep-down-to-the-core type of joy every day.

~ Joy, To Be or Not To Be ~

There are so many things that occur in our lives that could leave us with the question, "Joy, is it to be or not to be?" In pursuit of happiness, I have noticed that many struggle with being joy for many different reasons. One may say (1) "As long as there are people who do me wrong, I am not going to be joyful." One may say, (2) "Life is hard and that is why I can't be joyful." One may say, (3) "Joy is an emotion that erupts only when good things happen."

The philosophy of these sayings may seem to be sound, however are they the truth? What is truth and where can we find truth? ***John 17:17*** (KJV) Christ was praying to God the Father and He prayed, "Sanctify them through thy truth: thy word is truth." Since God's word is truth, to get answers, the sensible thing to do is to look to the *Bible.* It will set us apart from the weak, defenseless, dark effects of ignorance.

The *Bible* is one of the oldest books in the world and is one of the top-selling books in our nation. So many people own this popular book, but many remain Biblically illiterate and are incapable of applying God's word to their everyday living. Consequently, the number of people who do not know or buy into what the *Bible* says about joy is astounding. However, there is great news! ***Urban Joy*** is an excellent book to aid in studying foundational scriptures and putting into practice the ways of joy. ***II Timothy 2:15*** (KJV) directs us to "Study to show ourselves approved unto God, a workman that need not to be ashamed, rightly dividing the word of truth." The *Bible* is the word of Truth. The omniscient (all-knowing) God saw it fitting to leave us a guide. When we invest time in studying this guide, we will understand God's heart about life and the subject of joy. Understanding the heart of our creator concerning joy works twofold. We will eliminate falling into shameful positions and inviting havoc into our lives. We will also be encouraged to practice joy daily.

If you are one to say, **(1) As long as there are people who do me wrong, I am not going to be joyful**, I have much to say concerning that subject. God reveals in the *Bible* His attitude concerning those who do His people wrong. Our joy of living is never at the mercy of evildoers. We never have to fret because of them. God is a fierce Father and He makes it clear that He will defend His children who are being messed over. We can rejoice in His reassurance in ***Isaiah54:17*** (KJV)

"No weapon formed against you shall prosper" in ***I Chronicles 16:22*** (KJV) God declares a warning, "Touch not mine anointed and do my prophets no harm." In ***Psalm 89:22-23*** (TNIV) our omnipotent (all-powerful) God describes the benefits of belonging to Him and what He will do to our adversaries: "No enemy will get the better of him; no wicked person will oppress him. I will crush his foes before him and strike down his adversaries." Our joy can flow freely knowing that almighty God is our protector, defender and He never sleeps.

These scriptures remind me of a true story about what happened to Eddie, my Dad's mechanic. He was walking down a street in Camden, NJ, one day and unfortunately walked up on an unleashed pit bull. Threatened by his presence, the pit bull leaped to sink his teeth into Eddie. Right before the point of contact, Eddie sprayed mace directly into the dog's face and was about to run. The amazing thing that happened next stopped Eddie from running. He explained, never had he seen a dog do what that pit-bull did. Once hit with the mace, the dog froze in midair as his two front paws immediately covered his eyes. Still standing upright on his hind legs the dog briskly ran across the street and then comically down the street. Eddie was able to watch in awe as his defeated foe run away upright like a man yelping a few choice words in doggie language.

We can stand and watch God use His tactics to foil the plan of our enemies and watch them flee right before our eyes. Thus, no matter how evil a person's intentions, the Lord will protect us as we battle through their ungodly ways. ***Psalms 140:7*** (NLT) says, "O Sovereign Lord, the strong one who rescued me, you protected me on the day of battle." God will give us strategies and wisdom to use the right weapons of our warfare while in battle. You can believe that no matter what people say or do, God Almighty is watching, and says, "Vengeance is mine." ***(Romans 12:19)*** (KJV) We do not have to come up with our own strategies. Our orders will come from the headquarters of our Commander and Chief. I have learned to trust Him and look to Him for instructions. Every time I do it God's way, I come through victoriously and see the demise of my enemy.

Always look for what is truth, there you will find cloture

It is so much easier to let go of a matter in the realm of truth. If people lie on and lie to you, focus on what is true and not on the lie.

Dwelling on lies will only rustle up our pride and will promote anger and frustration. I remember a time when I was fourteen and still a virgin. I physically blossomed and people in the church (men and women) would comment on me being attractive. There was some jealousy that came with their comments. I remember a lie went throughout the church that I asked a grown man, my grandmother's neighbor, to take me home during a church concert because I was experiencing my monthly and did not feel well. They reported that I got in his vehicle and he and I were having sex in the back seat. When I heard this ridiculous lie, I laughed and hoped that people did not believe that nonsense. I only focused on the fact that I was a virgin . . . and the truth is what mattered.

Surprisingly, being so young, I handled that lie well. As time progressed, two adults came forward with a very troubled conscience. They apologized, stating that they started the rumor with intent to tarnish my reputation. Tarnishing my reputation was their goal because the pastor's son had begun to show an interest in me and they wanted his interest to turn towards their daughter. I forgave them, but that experience changed my life. I became convinced that there are some sick people in this world and they will do anything to get ahead no matter who it hurts, even in the church. Those two adults reaped what they sowed. Their reputation was tarnished. I also learned that *truth* really does prevail. We must focus on the truth and have great expectations that the Lord will come through for us. Knowing that the Lord will come through for us, will keep our joy flowing.

If people say all manner of things against you, meditate on ***Psalm 92:10-11*** (KJV*)* in which King David says,"….I shall be anointed with fresh oil. Mine eye also shall see my desire on mine enemies, and mine ears shall hear my desire of the wicked that rise against me." King David was anointed with fresh oil as a symbol of the Lord refreshing him in a right spirit. He did not decline his joy because his expectations were in God. David was aware of God's attitude about protecting His people, and he did not expect his enemies to get the best of him. Like King David, right in the midst of being tried, we can **Pray** and ask God to renew within us a right spirit and a clean heart. We should then reflect on God's promises with expectation to receive.

The **Flip Side** tells the other side of the story. When doing wrong, our consciences will not allow us to expect the promises of God. Before concluding that our joy not being expressed is due to people doing us wrong, we must examine our own ways to see if we are the cause of our own misery. What may seem to be an offense could very well be God using people or circumstances to put a finger on those characteristics in us that are not of Him. The law of sowing and reaping may be in effect. If we have sown by being manipulative, controlling, a meddler, judgmental, selfish, merciless, deceitful and falter in being credible, we are going to reap the repercussions of our actions. ***Proverbs 3:3-4*** (KJV) says, "Let not mercy and truth forsake thee: bind them about thy neck: write them upon the table of thine heart: So shalt thou find favor and good understanding in the sight of God and man." Something is wrong if we are finding that in every area of our life, we are leaving a trail of *disgruntled*, *angry*, *regretful*, *hurt* and *disappointed* people. Bad character creates this type of *enemy*, wreaks havoc and hinders the flow of joy. If we are finding that we have burned bridges across the map of our lives, something is wrong. If we are not finding favor and good understanding with men, we need to check ourselves. We should see the favor of God and man in every area of our lives. We should still see the favor and grace of God even while dealing with the wrongful deeds of others, including dealing with the consequences of our own mistakes. ***(Psalms 92:6)***

If we are not seeing God's favor and man's favor in our lives, we should check to see if we have been falling short on being merciful and if we are violating any truths. Someone shared with me that she was watching one of the daytime court reality shows. On that day, there was a Christian couple being sued by a woman. Prior to coming to court, the narrator reported that the couple sent threatening emails with statements that God said touch not my anointed and do my prophets no harm and some other threat that God was going to judge their accusers. As they continued to watch, the truth came out that the Christian couple owed this woman money and refused to pay her. They did not get favor from the judge nor did God keep them from the shame of being reprimanded on national television. In the couple's mind, no mercy was going to be shown to the woman that was bringing them to court. However, the judge's decision was entirely different. Every decision that we make, has a consequence whether good or bad. Knowing how to quote scripture is good but knowing how to live by the scriptures is best.

God is not going to side with us just because we know how to quote scripture. We must behave ourselves in accordance to God's word in order for us to expect His favor and man's favor in every area of our lives. Adults and even some children know that if a service is rendered, we have to *pay* the cost! ***Romans 13:8*** (KJV) says, "Owe no man anything...." Christians should not behave like thieves, crooks and poor stewards. As Christians, our charitable efforts and outreach projects do not excuse us from being good stewards. Being ambassadors for Christ does not give us diplomatic immunity and excuses us from having to pay for services rendered or paying back loans.

I work in sales. In the process of getting financed, people have to give their credit information. I have encountered several people who worked as leaders for the church, and their credit histories revealed that they paid no one back. I would want to mention their noble credible efforts of working for the Lord, but I could not because their credit histories would reveal something different. I am really grateful that all church leaders who come to my place of business are not like that. Their credibility matches their credit history. Examining our ways through the microscopic lens of God's word will expose and help eliminate those hidden degenerate things that corrupt our integrity and credibility. This process will also prevent us from making enemies which hinders our joy flowing.

Reneging Hinders Our Flow of Joy

Reneging on a promise will cause our credibility to falter and will create enemies as well. The joy of the Lord will not flow when we are wrong. People are not necessarily doing us wrong when they come after us because we owe them. Do not preempt possessions, supposedly by faith, and make good on payments. Real faith will manifest substance with integrity and good ethics. Egotistic greed for recognition, power and materialistic gain will manifest profit. But profitable gain does not necessarily materialize because of faith in God. **Don't get it twisted.** When God provides the substance we obtain, everything about it will be blessed and full of integrity. Our actions will not be that of a thief, and creditors will not be left with the regret of rendering their services. Creditors are not predators as some would suppose. They are actually a blessing because they have made things convenient for us in one way or another . . . however, with a fee.

I have worked in a ministry that owed just about everyone that rendered a service. From one project to another, the debt would escalate and both vendors and lenders would go unpaid. I have witnessed ministry department heads promise the church members that they would pay them back after charging large amounts on their credit cards. When it would come time to be paid back, it wouldn't happen. Once the projects were complete, over and over, I would hear the verbal agreement between the credit card holder and church officials change to a wave of words spoken to manipulate the agreement to being a sacrificial offering. Also, when events were canceled, deposits given were not given back. It would be said after the fact that they do not refund money given and the money would go to something never revealed or discussed. It was supposed to be understood that it went to God's work.

This type of behavior has produced a very unhealthy relationship between the church and many people. Unfortunately for some people, it has created a stumbling block in their minds towards the church and God. When we take advantage of people, we put a gulf between us and God. God is a God of righteousness and taking advantage of people is worthy of His punishment. ***I Thessalonians 4:6*** (NIV) says, "….no one should wrong or take advantage of a brother or sister. The Lord will punish all who commit such sins..." As a ministry if you cannot seem to get off of the ground concerning the growth of members and finances, search with good intent and purge all aspects of being incredulous in stewardship of both money and people.

If we do not have enough money to support our projects and or pay our bills, my advice is to take smaller steps, get more employment and come up with creative ideas to make money. Here's one suggestion for a creative idea that is a "money maker." Open a medical marijuana shop for glaucoma patients. You will be surprised at how many people have glaucoma. I'm just kidding. However with all jokes aside, we have to be good stewards and fervent in handling our business. ***(Romans 12:11)*** God does not want us so heavenly bound that we disrespect the earthly systems. When Christ walked this earth, He said in ***Matthew 22:21*** (KJV), "Render therefore unto Caesar the things which are Caesar's; and unto God the things that are God's." Caesar and his boys did some nasty perverted things, but Christ still wanted his disciples to respect the laws that they implemented. As long as we are not going against God's laws, we should do what is required of us.

Being credible does not hinder the flow of joy. Being credible also frees us up from fearful tactics such as relocating our vehicle to hide from the *Repo Villain,* or sic our dog on the *Creature from the Mail Lagoon* carrying certified mail in need of our signature, or tell our kids to lie to the *Collect-a-Debt Devil* trying to prevent that demon from tracking us down. When we are credible we do not have to slam the phone down or give the people who are doing their jobs a bad attitude because they are holding us accountable. Avoiding this type behavior will remove us from lineup of being an offender. Being credible will prevent us from creating jilted enemies -- and declining our joy.

Criminal Promises Hinder the Flow of Joy

Developing ***Urban Joy*** is inadvertently a way of eliminating petty things that hinder the flow of joy in our lives. Making "criminal promises" is petty and ultimately hinders the flow of joy. A criminal promise is making a commitment that we have no intention of keeping. We are not going to reap the favor of man or God by making criminal promises. Practicing behavior like this is deceitful and it lacks integrity and credibility. Working in sales, I have become numb to people who promise to hold to their appointment and then never show up. They don't even give a courtesy call to say that they are not going to make it. If we make promises, we should make an effort to keep them. I personally know that things will happen to hinder us from holding to our commitments. But a simple courtesy call and or an apology is the appropriate thing to do during those instances.

Setting an appointment and making a person wait an inconsiderate amount of time, is criminal. If we set an appointment, we should set it up for a time that we know that we can keep. Another thing, your voicemail greeting needs to be changed if you promise to call everyone back and have no intention of doing that. If you promise to be somewhere, the same principle applies. We must be men and women of our word. ***Psalms 19:14*** (KJV), King David prays to God saying**,** "Let the words of my mouth, and the meditation of my heart, be acceptable in thy sight, O Lord." If we live this prayer, our relationship with God and people will be so much better. We will find that the favor of God and man will follow us wherever we go. When we are favored, it indeed stirs our joy.

Managers, leaders, clergy, ministers, ambassadors of Christ, etc., if you make a promise, mean it. Prominent people in the church have made promises to me that I sincerely believed. But when it was time for them to deliver, they would not. They would not even mention that they promised. Walking in my Christian faith, I have noticed that some leaders say things because they sound good and they may be the right things to say. However, the fulfillment of their words never come to fruition. Some people would make pompous excuses for why they did not keep their word. Others would put the burden of the responsibility for the unfilled commitment on those to whom the promise was made. Regardless of our status, we are all responsible for holding to the words that we speak. We should write things down and set up various reminders that would help us to remember. We must care about considering others. It is **criminal** for us to make a promise and then not take any responsibility for keeping the promise, especially as followers of Christ. "People don't care how much you know until they know how much you care." (John Maxwell)

Is your credibility shot? Do you have a problem with people trusting or believing you? Just take some time and look back on your actions. If your actions have proven to be criminal, you must change if you want a better reputation. Do not make promises if you are extremely busy. Say things like, "I am not sure if I can" or, "Can you check back with me?" or *hush* and do not make a promise at all. Sometimes people are not looking for anything unless we open our mouths and give them something to expect.

I have seen leaders have major rebuke sessions or preach angry sermons because they no longer feel the admonition of their people. From my experience, much of the people's discontent is gravely from unfulfilled promises made by the leader. Leaders of excellence do not bully people. Excellent leaders are honored and respected because of their good ethics and good fruit (successes). Overall I have found that less energy is exerted when we simply humble ourselves, apologize, make fewer promises, and be accountable to the promises that we make. ***1 Corinthians 2:15*** (KJV) says, "But he that is spiritual judgeth all things, yet he himself is judged of no man." It exemplifies strong character to judge our own actions. When you are credible and do not make "criminal" promises, you will not be judged by anyone for a promise that you did not keep. Our relationships will flourish when we exercise this principle in church, at work, with our families, with our friends and in business. Relationships that flourish in credibility are like a stream, and the current of joy flows through that stream unhindered.

Blind Spots Hinders the Flow of Joy

We all have blind spots in how we handle people. Ultimately these blind spots can create enemies. Blind spots are inoperative ways about ourselves that we don't see. These ineffective ways spill over into how we handle people. They are character flaws that form a dam preventing the flow of joy in our relationships. The perfect exercise to test and reveal what's inside of us, is working with people. Our blind spots may cause us to experience disapproval, exclusion, rejection and chastisement. To correct blind spots, we first must be made aware of them. We cannot see our blind spots (hence the term *blind*). People must tell us. It is going to take humility to receive what they have to say as well as correcting our behavior to change.

Early in my Christian walk, I had a "victim mentality." I was one of those people always crying about somebody doing me wrong. But all along, it was I who was doing me wrong. I just didn't see it. As a babe in Christ, I thought I was purposely excluded from doing special things with my former pastor's wife. However, I had an unpredictable temperament and was disrespectful at times. Until I curtailed my behavior, quite naturally I was not on top of the list of those who she could safely put her trust in. The red carpet is not going to be rolled out for us if our behavior is not red-carpet behavior. I had to accept that I needed to change and I had to stop blaming others for treating me badly when I was the offender. When I changed, my positions in the ministry blossomed. As time progressed, whenever she traveled, I traveled with her. I was one of the individuals that was included in her ministry and personal agenda.

No one is configured to handle everyone perfectly. We need to learn, as well as change to properly handle people that come into our lives. It is never too late to change. Instead of acting ugly when I felt some sort of opposition from people, I developed a skill of handling matters a lot better. I also developed a skill of winning people over, especially if they do not seem to immediately take to me. I have come to a place in my life where I respect something that Jeff, one of my former managers in sales and now a good friend would quote Ron White, who said, "You can't fix stupid. Stupid will always be stupid. The definition will never change." I have come to realize that there are people that will not like you for no apparent reason. There are brutish people who will not change for anything or anybody. I have accepted that I cannot change the ways of those people. However, it is my personal conviction to remove my blind spots of poor character that are revealed about me. Instead of trying to tweak my stupid behavior, I have decided to stop being stupid and change.

In the automotive industry, manufacturers have invented many devices and gadgets to help motorists with vehicular blind spots. We greatly need people in our lives to function like a device that mirrors the areas we do not see. They will help prevent the crashing and colliding in relationships that happen as a result of blind spots. Ultimately we will have a better flow of joy in our relationships. Regardless of our status in life, from the most humble to the greatest, we should always stay open to change and try to get better at interacting with people. During conflict, people will tell us how they see us. We need to have an open ear because **truth is revealed in conflict**. We cannot be so caught up in only seeing the flaws of others. God has given others the same optical lens to see our flaws no matter our opinion of ourselves. Humility is the key ingredient of accepting our blind spots and changing to ultimately interact with people expressing joy.

Religious Arrogance Hinders the Flow of Joy

As humans, we make mistakes with each other every day. The frailties of human behavior can cause much pain. In some instances, the pain is inflicted by the blows of arrogance. Many no longer enjoy the true blessings of attending church because they have been wounded by church members and leaders. They forsake assembling in the house of God because of poor representation of Christ. Christ's main opposition came from those who held prominent positions in the temple. I would like to interject that religious, ritualistic people of the church, are not God. If their behavior is critical and judgmental, do not be intimated by their opinions. God is greater than their tongue lashings and criticisms. His thoughts are not their opinions. Do not be governed by opinions of people; they are common. An acquaintance once made a funny-but-true statement: "An opinion is like a butthole; everyone has one."

From my observation, the only people that Christ put a whipping to in the Bible, were the religious. ***(Mathew 21:12)*** The pompous, critical sticklers of the Mosaic Law got rebuked. Christ forgave -- and healed --

liars, prostitutes, adulterers, thieves and the like. Once forgiven, he would instruct some of them to go and sin no more. Christ's purpose for coming was to destroy the works of the adversary. ***(I John 3:8).*** He did not come to criticize, condemn and/or ostracize people. No matter who the religious leaders think of themselves, I am certain they are not God.

We have to be steadfast in trusting in God, not in people. Doing so enables us to see past the bad behavior of people and clearly hear God's instructions on how to handle matters. Furthermore, the difference between their behavior and God's is evident. *With God exclusively on the thrones of our hearts, we are empowered to joyfully handle the many disappointing actions of people.*

God being on the throne of my heart helped me to only focus on those things that are most needful in my life (my relationship with Him, my divine purpose, my family, friends and career.) Anything outside of those important factors in my life can go back from whence it came.

When God is Lord of our hearts,
we are never depressed.

When God is at the helm controlling our life, going to His house of worship will not be a thing of the past. God will keep us on course of keeping our priorities straight in Him. While fulfilling our destinies, our focus on Him will shield us from the poison darts and spurs of the religious and we will of a certainty flow in joy.

With my whole heart, I have done much for pastors. All that I have done did not stop them from doing some hurtful things. I made the mistake of putting them on the throne of my heart. I realized in my downtrodden, wounded state, I had unfortunately placed people where God should be. In my downtrodden wounded state, God revealed to me that my heart belongs to Him and from my heart He will always guide me to forgive, release, love and live. God's word says, "Above all else, guard your heart, for everything you do flows from it." ***Proverbs 4:23*** (TNIV). With God reigning in my heart, I will never make the mistake of putting people in His place ever again. If ministers say hurtful things, remember they are not God; they are human. If ministers do immoral things, they are not God they are human. If ministers do things that lack credibility, again I say, they are not God, they are human.

As far back as I could remember, I have seen exposure in the media about religious leaders doing things that the whole world knows are wrong. They are imprisoned because of offenses like tax evasion and pedophilia. Their homosexual lovers or women in the church have brought to light their sexual misconduct, as their disgraced spouses are on the sidelines, shocked and confused. They have led a mass of people to commit suicide by drinking a beverage laced with cyanide. None of those actions are good or of God. They are not a representation of Christ. The hearts of mankind is deceived in believing that perverted passions and lust are admissible in the world of decency as long as it is covered up. Not so. It is no secret to God that we operate in deception. ***Jeremiah 17:9*** (KJV) says, "The heart is deceitful above all things, and desperately wicked." However, we all have Christ as a Savior and a merciful God who has unconditional love for us. "And he is the propitiation for our sins: and not for ours only, but also for the sins of the whole world." ***I John 2:2*** (KJV*)*

Romans 3:23 (KJV) says, "All men have sinned and come short of the Glory of God. If we say that we have no sin, we deceive ourselves, and the truth is not in us." ***I John 1:8-9*** (KJV*)* "If we confess our sins, he is faithful and just to forgive us our sins, and to cleanse us from all unrighteousness." God has not distinguished in His word that some sins are okay and some aren't. Sin is sin. The difference is that some sins have greater repercussions than others. Some sins do more damage than others and the consequences are more severe. God will forgive our transgressions because of Christ. God is holy and He is glorious. God knows no sin. He rightfully maintains His position of honor. Therefore, man and God can never be on the same plateau. No man comes even close to God's level of holiness, consistency and honor. With God as the only one on the throne of our heart, we can be assured of never being steered in the wrong direction. Many turn away from God because of the behavior of others. We have to be determined not to blame God for what humans do. If a drunk driver gets behind a wheel, he can kill. If a pedophile is left alone with a child, he will hurt or possibly even kill the child. If a deranged, sadistic person gets a weapon, he will kill. If a thief is given the opportunity, he will steal. If a pompous, religious, ritualistic judgmental person has breath, he will criticize and judge.

It is not God who transgresses against us. Sometimes we want to blame God for what people say and do. I personally know that sometimes we can also get so caught up in ministry functions that the ability to distinguish the difference between God and man gets clouded.

I remember being told that everything that comes out of my pastor's mouth is God. I remember being told that everything that the pastor does is God. So when that pastor would be misinformed and uphold a lie, publicly humiliate me, do or say things that were mean, hurtful, disrespectful, degrading, manipulating, and anger driven, I would go into a state of confusion. My heart reminded me of a true, loving, merciful, and caring God full of grace, however the words spoken from the representative of God would be the opposite. Consequently, I battled the feeling of being condemned, and unloved by God. I remember feeling God was angry with me; however, in actuality, it wasn't God who was angry . . . it was the pastor.

I firmly believe in ***Proverbs 3:12*** (KJV) which states, "God will chasten those who He loves." God will correct those things that are not right in our lives. No chastisement feels good. However, God's chastening does not leave us beaten down, humiliated or feeling like He doesn't love us. God will bring to our attention those areas in our lives that need to be corrected by way of scriptures. His instructions will not be riddled with man's philosophy and opinion. God's correction will come with instructions in righteousness delivered through the fruit of the Spirit of God. ***2 Timothy 3:16*** (KJV) says, "All scripture is given by inspiration of God, and is profitable for doctrine, for reproof, for correction, for instruction in righteousness." God's spiritual leaders are much like personal trainers. They will take us further than what we would do on our own. They will also encourage us to stop doing the things that work against us. Even though their training can be very uncomfortable, as well as, takes us out of our comfort zone, we know that their training is good for us. When the correction is given God's way, our convictions and efforts to changed will not be displaced. Our focus will not be on what more I can do to get on a human's good side but rather how to please our Heavenly Father. ***Colossians 3:23***(KJV) says, "And whatsoever ye do, do it heartily, as to the Lord, and not unto men."

When we are joyous, people will always leave our presence better even after correcting them. Joyous leaders who correct and set order, do not damage their people. Their people are left with the sense of love and joy. ***I John 6-8*** (KJV) says, "Beloved let us love one another for to love is of God and everyone that loves is born of God and knows God and he that loves not knows not God for God is love." Also ***I Corinthians 13:4*** (ESV) give us a clear picture of what love looks like in the eyes of God and it says, “Love is patient and kind; love does not envy or boast; it is not arrogant or rude. It does not insist on its own way; it is not irritable or resentful: it does not rejoice at wrongdoing, but rejoices with the truth. Love bears all things, believes all things, hopes all things, endures all things." So, you see, God's love does not ostracize, criticize, condemn or verbalize hurtful, mean things.

Saying, “I love you” after verbally damaging people is not proof of love being demonstrated at all. Using scripture to ostracize, criticize and or condemn is not demonstrating love either. Love is felt when it is truly demonstrated God’s way. True love will never leave people damaged but it will make sure people are healed, whole and helped. God is the ultimate representation of love. He is the epitome of love. No matter what we have done, God sent his Son for our forgiveness, deliverance and healing. He did it because He loves us, not because we deserve it. Concluding on this subject, I leave you with this: Remember that people are not God, they are human; only allow God to reign on the throne of your heart and love people despite their shortcomings; remember that no human being has a heaven or hell to put us in. This is a sure formula that will help you not to spiral down into negative emotions because of the arrogance of others and a sure formula for ***Urban Joy*** to freely flow through us.

Bad-mouthing People Hinders the Flow of Joy

God’s expression of love manifesting through us should eliminate our desire to bad-mouth people. Bad-mouthing is talking negative about a person through negative emotions. We may not always like the things that people say or do. However, we must realize that bad-mouthing people and joy do not flow together. Bad-mouthing people also creates enemies. If a discussion is needed concerning the negative things that people say or do, or, if they do something that we particularly do not prefer, the discussion should be done through the intent of looking for the best solution that will manifest peace and righteousness. It should not be done to damage but to gain wisdom. People should always leave our presence better. People will never leave our presence better if we backbite or talk negative about them.

We must realize that whatever we *say* will *spray* our environment. Bad-mouthing people carry an aroma like wearing cologne. When we spray ourselves with cologne, as time elapses, we no longer smell the fragrance, however, others can smell it. If we spray negativity and think that it has dissipated, others will still sense the stench of it. Even when we think we have concealed it, people will still sense it. They sense the murmurings that we house about them. I can account for the times of walking in a room where there would be a group of people and would sense that there was something wrong. It would seem like something stank even though they frothed a polite greeting. Unfortunately, that group would be Christians. The negative things thought and or said had left its residue. ***Galatians 5:15*** (KJV) was written to Christians and it says, "But if ye bite and devour one another, take heed that ye be not consumed one of another." God made sure ***Galatians 5:15*** was in His word for us Bible toting, scripture quoting, glory Hallelujah-ing Christians to watch our mouths. The effects of bad-mouthing people can consume the hearts of people if it's not corrected.

Bad-mouthing people is very harmful. It is a real problem that will cause us to decline joy. If we do not want to create enemies, we must refrain from that type of behavior. ***Urban Joy*** will cause us to be joyous even when people behave in a manner that we do not prefer. We do not have to speak bitterly or say hateful things. ***I John 2:9*** (NIV) *s*ays, "Anyone who claims to be in the light but hates a brother or sister is still in the darkness." Instead of being hateful by backbiting, we can be fair, firm and consistent. By being fair, firm and consistent, we do not have to resort to bad-mouthing people. We can be fair by treating people fairly even if they are not part of our clique or group, or behave the way we think that they should. We can be firm by not wavering on the standards and principles that are wholesome and helpful. We can be consistent in maintaining a fresh, clean atmosphere by being pleasant. ***Proverbs 16:24*** (KJV) says, "Pleasant words are as a honeycomb, sweet to the soul and health to the bones." Many of us are very careful about selecting healthy choices of what goes into our mouths. Why not be careful about being selective concerning what comes out of our mouths?

I thought it was hilarious when my daughter Angie shared with me a chilling experience that she had with her husband, who is gentle and kind by nature. Early in getting to know him, she explained that she felt chills go up her spine a few times when her husband would abruptly interrupt her from bad-mouthing someone. It was as if his abrupt words of disapproval would karate chop her throat while she was speaking. She explained that she would feel "busted." She couldn't justify her actions because she knew he was right. We all need to have someone in our lives to help us like my son-in-law. I appreciate him when he helps me. Bad-mouthing people can be subtle and we think that we can sneak and weave it into our wholesome way of living and get away with it. We think that it does not cause any damage. We think that we can do it and still maintain being joyful. However, that is far from being truth. We wear bad-mouthing people like we wear cologne. The evidence of it will be apparent offsetting the good smelling fragrance of joy

Many of us spend good money making sure we smell good. Why not spend good time making sure the things that come out of our mouths smell just as good as the designer cologne that we wear? In order to successfully maintain a good fragrance about us, there is something that we must do. We must come to terms that people are going to do things differently and will do things that we do not prefer. Bridling our tongue is the first step in coming to terms with this bad habit. I put a bridle on my tongue by not saying things concerning people like "I don't like, I can't stand, I can't believe, Why can't they? Idiots, Morons, Retards, Bastards, they make me sick. They get on my nerves. Who do they think they are?, I am sick of them all," and not to mention all of the *curse words* that could be spewed out. All these phrases are a set up for murmuring and/or backbiting in which we should refrain from doing as instructed in ***II Corinthians 12:20***. If you are one to say these things, I am sure you go on without examining how you feel after you muttered them. Your atmosphere and your insides are not fresh. You may be conformed to think that you feel better when you talk like that. If you can be true to yourself, your insides are downright funky. You do not have good spiritual hygiene. You are not joyful, or positive. Turn over a new leaf. If you cannot say anything good, say nothing and control your thoughts if you want to live a quality joyful life. If you do not want a joyful quality life, just keep on doing what you do. But please understand that we cannot cry and blame anyone for our drama filled negative life but ourselves.

It is pleasing to our heavenly Father that we control our tongue. We should all endeavor to do things to please God. He has done sooo much for us and loves us sooo much. The least that we could do is try. If we do not have any respect for God and the things of God, we will continue to use foul language with justification. If we want to respect God and the things of God, we should adopt King David's prayer in

Psalms 19:14 (KJV) "Let the words of my mouth, and the meditation of my heart, be acceptable in thy sight O Lord."

Cursing (using foul language) is unacceptable and considered bad-mouthing people. I know many Christians who have a different view than I do concerning cursing. Dr. Bill Hamon, the founder of Christian International and author helped me to break my habit of cursing. As a keynote speaker at a conference, he reproved us about cursing and cursing people by saying words to this effect, "Cursing did not derive from God's Holy Spirit, it is the Devil's language and we should be ashamed being vessels of God freely speaking for the Devil." Dr. Bill Hamon's message pricked my heart and caused me to connect my cursing to representing something evil. The Devil isn't the man with a red suit with horns who whispers little fun tantalizing things in our ear. He is the epitome of evil. He hates all of mankind and the good of mankind. I am talking hate with a capital HATE.

Let me give you some examples of the Devil's evil hate which is part of why I stopped representing him by cursing: A friend of mine who is a former police officer worked in a department that he had to watch as evidence a video recorded by a pedophile rapist sexually assaulting a very small little girl. The evil-possessed man recorded in pleasure as he brutally and mercilessly caused external and internal harm to the child. My friend said the blood-curdling screams of the little girl and seeing something so evil changed his life. Only something that is pure evil would do something like that. Do we want to represent someone like that? I don't think so. What about the evil that horrified our nation by crashing into the twin towers in New York, killing thousands of people, or the evil that went into a classroom with an automatic weapon and mercilessly killed several five- and six-year-old innocent little children? Dr. Bill Hamon's message caused me not to want to have anything to do with something so evil and foul. Ultimately my habit of cursing or using foul language was broken.

James 3:9-13 (NLT***)*** speak on God's opinion on how we use our tongue to curse people and praise Him: "Sometimes it praises our Lord and Father, and sometimes it curses those who have been made in the image of God. And so blessings and cursing come pouring out of the same mouth. Surely, my brothers and sisters, this is not right! Does a spring of water bubble out with both fresh water and bitter water? Does a fig tree produce olives, or a grapevine produce figs? No, and you can't draw fresh water from a salty spring. If you are wise and understand God's ways, prove it by living an honorable life, doing good works with the humility that comes from wisdom."

God's word clearly is telling us, if we claim to be wise and full of knowledge then show it by our conversation with humility in Christ. Christ did not murmur, backbite, curse and or complain. Christ came to *destroy the works of the devil* ***(I John 3:8).*** He did not come to partner with the devil and neither should we with our mouths. Christ spoke those things that He heard His Father speak. ***John 8:28*** (KJV) Jesus says, "… I do nothing of myself; but as my Father hath taught me, I speak these things." To allow Christ to work through us, it will take discipline to speak the word that God taught us. It will also take humility and obedience to position ourselves to learn God's ways and live out God's ways. Christians are followers of Christ. We as Christians should stop making excuses for being foul in speaking and still call ourselves followers of Christ. We are *not* following Christ when we curse. Every time we speak we represent someone or something. Think about that. Who, in our heart of hearts, do we want to represent? If our answer is Christ, we must clean up our acts and stop being spiritually funky. A quality of living in joy flows freely when we stop ourselves from speaking hatefully, bitterly and being evil by bad-mouthing people.

Another observation that I have made is that people bad-mouth people because of minding other people's business. Minding people's business for the sake of gossip will never be good. Minding people's business for the sake of feeling more superior will never be good. Both of these courses of action will lead to bad-mouthing people. Sometimes we speak concerning the affairs of others not knowing the full details. We cast judgment and make a determination that is far from the truth. It is amazing how troubled we get minding the business of others and we say some pretty ugly things about those people. I know people who get in a tizzy about other people's business. They get into debates or arguments about other people's business. God has a solution for this type behavior. ***I Thessalonians 4:11*** (KJV) says, "Study to be quiet and do your own business..." If you ask me, God is telling us to *Be Quiet* and *Mind Our Own Business*! God knows we really are happiest when we mind our own business and refrain from bad-mouthing people. Don't you want the happier things in life? Refraining from bad-mouthing people is a good start of removing the corrupt clutter in our soul making more room for the fullness of joy.

Concerning the subject, **(1) As long as there are people who do me wrong, I am not going to be joyful**, much has been said. However, I conclude by saying that we can still maintain our joy regardless. Our heavenly Father is ever present to deliver us from evildoers. He will protect us and refresh us while in battle. We do not have to consume our day and our thoughts with the horrible actions of others. We have the privilege of fulfilling our day with the promises of our Father. Every day we will have the privilege of living our divine purpose.

Now on the *Flip Side*, we cannot cry "wolf" if we are being the wolf. We cannot cry that we are being victimized if our actions are causing it. We must stop creating enemies if we want our joy to flow. We must stop short-circuiting our relationship with God, thereby deceiving ourselves by thinking that our unethical behavior will reap the happiness that we desperately seek. Regardless of age, it is never too late to change. We cannot expect God to have our backs if we are being the offenders. We cannot expect the promises of God, if we are wrong. To live out the true revelation of ***Urban Joy***, we have to be responsible and align ourselves with being credible. We must cooperate with effective ways of handling people. We must allow God -- and God only -- to reign in our hearts. We must love people and bridle our tongues, keeping our minds, wills and emotions free from the clutter of bad thinking and speaking. Freeing ourselves of these ways ultimately emanates a joyful lifestyle.

If you are one to say, **(2) "Life is hard and that is why I can't be joy,"** it is imperative that we allow our faith in the truth to set us free.

In truth, there will be some harsh things in life that we will face. Imagine that we can go to church twenty-four hours a day and seven days a week, or live like Anna in the *Bible* and pray day and night in the temple. It does not matter; harsh things are still going to happen from the richest to the poorest. None of us live in a glass bubble. Although experiencing hardship doesn't mean that we have to live a hard life. ***Matthew 11:28-30*** (KJV) Jesus says, "Come unto me, all ye that labor and are heavy laden, and I will give you rest. Take my yoke upon you, and learn of me, for I am meek and lowly in heart: and ye shall find rest unto your souls. For my yoke is easy, and my burden is light." This promise reveals that we can turn every hardship over to the Lord. He will give us rest. Hardship can be felt going through adversities, challenges, trials, temptations, tribulations, sickness, death, etc.

So, how do we mentally and emotionally release ourselves from the grip of hardship? How do we release it to someone that we cannot see or touch? How to do it is simple:

- Write down all of the things that are not giving you rest.
- Create an altar in your mind no matter where you are.
- See yourself taking everything you have written to Him. Say, "Lord, I give it all to you"
- Place it down at the altar in your mind.
- Once you have given it to the Lord, trash what you have written down. The Lord has it.

When you go to think about those things that you have given Him, just say to yourself, "No, I will not dwell on it. I have given it to the Lord and I will continue to rest." Then demonstrate your faith by expecting Him to guide your every footstep successfully.

Matthew 11:28-30 (KJV), Christ also instructs us to "learn of Him." When we learn ***Hebrews 7:25*** (KJV) that tells us how *He is forever praying for us*, we take ourselves off the hook that we do not pray enough. Who better can pray more consistently and more accurately than our Lord? When we learn ***Romans 8:34:*** *"He bore our sins and we no longer have to walk in condemnation,"* we will stop trying to fix ourselves and just allow his words to take root in our hearts. When we learn "He is in touch with our feelings of weaknesses" ***(Hebrews 4:15)*** we will know that no matter what our weaknesses are, He doesn't shy away from us like we are so horrible. He stays right there with us to make us stronger; when we learn that "He is a friend that will never leave us" ***(Hebrews 13:5***) regardless of our weaknesses, flaws, handicaps and or problems, we will stop wasting time beating ourselves up. We will embrace that He is always there to help us through our difficulties; and when we learn that "We can throw all of our cares on Him because He cares for us" ***(I Peter 5:7),*** we will rest and get a sense of security that the Lord qualifies to handle all of the things that we have given to Him.

We all have given much time in learning about all sorts of things in life. Why not learn the information that will bring us rest, peace and joy? I assure you, seek and you will find many churches/study groups, resources in the book stores and so many other ways to learn about the care, concern and promises of God. You will find that the more you learn, the fewer burdens you will carry in your life. You will be carefree with an understanding that the Lord is carrying your load. You will discover that living a hard life will be foreign to you.

On the other hand, **life will be hard if you transgress repeatedly** (having no regard for wisdom and truth). ***Proverbs 13:15*** (KJV) says, "The life of a transgressor is hard." When we act in violation of God, others and ourselves, we clearly do not choose the wisest avenue of handling a matter. It is wise not to breach boundaries that secure our life's foundation.

Choosing wisdom will always bring you happiness in the long run

Proverbs 3:13 (KJV) says, "Happy is the man that finds wisdom and the man that get understanding." When transgressions are committed, wisdom is exiled and truth is wrongfully imprisoned. We all have transgressed. When we transgress, most of the time, we are aware of our wrong. However, there are some transgressions that fall under our radar. These subtle transgressions cause a lot of damage. Many of us do not realize that *worrying, fear* and a *lack of faith*, are three acts of transgressing that will make life hard. These three behavior patterns trigger a chain of actions that causes us to transgress against God, ourselves, others, and cause us to decline joy.

I will touch on the three areas and will start by exposing **worrying**.

When we worry, we absolutely positively do not trust God

Regardless of the confessions of faith that may proceed out of our mouths prior to worrying, we have totally given into our circumstance. ***Philippians 4:6-7*** (NLT) says, "Don't worry about anything; instead, pray about everything. Tell God what you need, and thank Him for all He has done. Then you will experience God's peace, which exceeds anything we can understand. His peace will guard your hearts and minds as you live in Christ Jesus." We serve a God that desires to take every worry from us and replace our worries with peace. Living in peace substantiates a quality life.

A worrier already knows that it does not help matters at all to worry. If ongoing, it could make you physically ill. Hypertension, ulcers, and chronic depression many times are as a result of worrying. Worrying accelerates the aging process, it causes eating disorders and contorts our facial expressions. Worrying affects our households and everything around us. Worrying brings the meanness out of people. Why not trust God? Why not trust someone who has created the Earth, mankind and all the miraculous beauty that we see? Being joy is so much better for us than worrying. Worrying is an enemy of joy. Get out of the driver's seat of your life and literally trust and know that God is "an excellent driver." as quoted in the movie "Rain Man" by Dustin Hoffman. God will not drive you to a cigarette to get the peace and rest that you want and need. He will not drive you to get a drink or pop pills to get the peace and rest that you need. He will drive you right into His arms of comfort and rest. "His peace will guard your hearts and minds as you live in Christ Jesus." ***Philippians 4:17***

There are many things that we give thought to that may leave us in question. For instance, Is the economy going to get better or is it going to get worse? Is my job going to be threatened? Is my 401 K going to be there when I need it? Am I going to get Social Security when I am of age? Will I be able to afford a car and insurance with gas prices escalating? What is this world going to be like for my children and children's children? Am I going to have enough money for the things that I want and need in life? The list goes on and on. Many of us just don't leave these questions in thought mode. We worry. ***(Matthew 6:25-33)*** (NLT) says, "…Why do you have so little faith? So don't worry about these things... These things dominate the thoughts of unbelievers, but your heavenly Father already knows all your needs. Seek the Kingdom of God above all else, and live righteously, and he will give you everything you need." We can rest because God promises to give us everything we need if we look to Him above all else and live right. All we need is faith to combat the depleting, troubling, draining, and sickening effects of worrying. Worrying forfeits the true experience of ***Urban Joy***. Being joy instead of a worrier is a healthy place mentally, socially, spiritually and physically. It is a delightful place that allows God the opportunity to make good on His promises.

Concerning **fear**, I have not met anyone who was not afraid of someone or something at one time or another. The expression of fear, like being startled, is harmless. Many times our startled reaction gives us a good chuckle. Many times we overcome our fears in a fairly quick manner. However, if not, fear can be very harmful, grave, dark . . . causing death to anything and everything in its path. Fear occurs when we don't understand or cannot control a matter. Our ignorance and lack of control can sink our minds into a black hole of fearful thoughts. Our dreams, talents, aspirations, goals, relationships and even our lives are seized, and our minds are tormented if fear has a grip on us.

The online *Free Dictionary by Farlex* defines *fear* as being "an unpleasant emotion caused by the belief that someone or something is dangerous likely to cause pain or threat. Fear is the unpleasant emotional stress caused by anticipation or awareness of danger. A phobia is a persistent abnormal and irrational fear of a specific thing or situation that compels one to avoid." Some of the common phobias that I have encountered with people are acrophobia (fear of cats) and claustrophobia (fear of being in a narrow or close space). I worked in a geographical area where people's teeth were rotting away because some suffered from dentophobia (fear of a dentist). Another common phobia is nyctophobia (fear of the dark). I know some children who suffered from pharmacophobia (fear of taking medicine or drugs). I have helped some women who suffered from eremophobia (fear of being alone). During our adolescent days my brother and I tormented by sister, Yolanda, horribly by chasing her around the house with the very thing that frightened her. She suffered from ichthyophobia (fear of fish).

I am not proud to mention that I have been fearful of creepy crawly things (hepetophobia) and spiders (arachnophobia). I would become irrational when sharing the same space with such creatures. The threat of one of them touching my skin, hair or clothing (or anyone else's) in my presence would set me off. Every nerve in my body would seemingly quiver. One time I dreamed that a spider dropped down in a friend's face, and I fainted while trying to warn her. When I awoke I thought to myself, "How can I be so afraid that I pass out in a dream?" From that experience, I realized that my feelings went beyond just being squeamish; it revealed that I had a problem.

On one occasion, I almost ended up in my daughter's lap while she was driving. I was trying to get away from a spider pretty big in size. As I tried to brush it away from me with paper, that spider had nothing of it. He was moving towards me like he was doing a test run for "Nas-spider 300." At a rapid pace, the spider's objective was to crawl above my head. All I could think to do was to get away from it. I did not take into account that my daughter was driving in traffic. I was, literally, almost completely on top of her. My reaction could have caused an accident. Thank God my daughter keeps a cool head and is skillful in driving. She safely pulled into a nearby parking lot. I lost my credibility of being "Supermom." All my cool, calm, and Jesus is my refuge mentally went out the window as I jumped out of the car *screaming!*

In my rational state of mind, I realized that I could not behave like that. I could have caused my daughter, other motorists and I harm. I have been working on getting better when a spider and I share the same space. I have seen some progress. They hang around my outdoor flowers while I am gardening. I see them in my home. When I see them, I talk to myself without freaking out. I do not like looking at them because they still "oooooffh ill-lagalagah" give me the willies. However, I tell myself that I am greater than the spider, and that I have more power and control than the spider does. I feel even more empowered when I get a broom, which gives me two arms' lengths in dealing with those little suckers

But on a more serious note, fear has caused much hatred, bloodshed, segregation and death in our nation and the world.

Fear is the root of prejudice; the path to paranoia, the bread of lunacy. Fear is the bed of a coward; the boa that constricts confidence; the cloak of a quitter

Fear has conquered powerful, talented, brilliant people. If we are not careful, fear will infiltrate our minds and will asphyxiate our sound thinking.

I was watching ID (Investigation Discovery, a cable/satellite TV station) one evening. This particular show was a reenactment of the true story of a millionaire. He became well off because of his athletic success. His son, who was also athletically talented, was diagnosed with cancer. He went through the necessary treatments and had begun to look and feel much better. The fear of seeing his strong, talented son die of cancer took the millionaire to the black hole of fearful thoughts. His son who went to bed happy one night, never saw the next day. His father shot and killed him in his sleep. He then went to his beautiful, mansion, master bedroom and splattered his blood and brains all over it with the same gun. The saddest and most tragic part of this whole story is that the son's autopsy revealed he was cancer-free. With all his money and both his and his son's talent, the father allowed fear to overtake his sound judgment. Fear blinded him from seeing that his son was doing better. He ended their lives never seeing the day to rejoice that his son was healed.

II Timothy 1:7 (KJV) says, "God did not give us the spirit of fear but of power and of love, and of a sound mind." Unless we are told, we are not born knowing what our privileges are. God wants us to know our privileges. We just need to take the time to study the scriptures. The scriptures let us know that we are given so much unmerited favor. We are privileged beyond understanding. When in relationship with God, we must thoroughly understand that He is not the author of fear. We are privileged because anything that is not from God, we do not have to accept. "For ye have not received the spirit of bondage again to fear but ye have received the spirit of adoption whereby we cry 'Abba, Father' (Daddy)." ***(Romans 8:15)*** We can call on our heavenly Father about anything that we fear. Our Daddy has given us the same *power* that He used to raise Jesus from the dead. We have the power to free ourselves from the fear that binds us, restrict us, consume us, asphyxiate us, and cause us to do some senseless harmful things.

Joy is nowhere to be found when we are bound by fear. Operating in fear, we give it permission to disable our power and as a result we say and do some crazy things. We inhibit our true potential, abilities, and sound judgment. In God we have the power to say, "No more!" to whatever ails us and then watch our fear fade away. Our sound minds and the love for ourselves will position us to get the help that we need from our heavenly Father and/or medical attention if that's what we need. We don't have to cope with fear. Fear is an enemy of joy. We will not live quality lives by being fearful day in and day out. Joy and fear do not coexist in the same rink; one will knock the other out. Whichever one we feed with our thoughts will be the victor. Knowledge put into action appropriately TKOs (totally knocks out) fear, and we joyfully rein as champion.

In sales, I often work with people who need a vehicle badly but faces a fear of making a decision (decidophobia). Regardless of the sound advice given, their fear would paralyze their decision-making, and they would leave without a vehicle. I have heard true stories of people who were threatened while having a gun in their hand. They would be so frightened that they would drop the power in their hand and would either run away or stand defenselessly.

My brother Steve told me a joke that is a good example of this type of fear:

One morning a husband decided that he was not going to church with his wife. He decided that he was going to go hunting. The wife was not in agreement but she could not talk him out of going. With his gun and joy of hunting, he set off to the woods. He sat in a perfect hidden place to prey on Bambi's cousin. Patiently waiting for awhile, he suddenly heard twigs snapping and breaking behind him. He quickly turned around and was facing a big grizzly bear heading straight for him. Scared out of his wits, he dropped his gun and took off running. *Bruuuff, Bruuff, Bruuff* was the sound the bear made as he was gaining on him. While running, the man turned to see how close the bear was, tripped over a stump and fell to the ground. The bear was so close that the man started to pray, "O God, O God, forgive me for not going to church and God, please let the bear be a Christian bear!" The bear caught up to him, stopped and stood up on his hind legs, slobbering, breathing heavy and glaring at the man. He then strangely put his huge paws together, bowed his head and prayed, "Father, thank you for this food that I am about to receive".

This joke uncovers the truth of how when we come face-to-face with adversity, challenges, danger, etc., we don't consider the power that we have but choose to choke in fear. This joke also comically tells the tale of how we can say and do some unsound things while facing our troubles.

As a young city girl, in the summertime I enjoyed visiting my Aunt Girt who lived in a rural town named Sicklerville, NJ. During one visit, she told me a story that her next-door neighbor had shared with her. He started the story by explaining that while cutting his grass he had seen another neighbor walking along the road, finely dressed. He described in detail her hat, sleeveless top and beautiful long, flowing skirt. As she was walking, a car approached on the same side of the road. For some strange reason, the woman jumped right in front of the moving vehicle. The car screeched to a halt, but not before coming into contact with the woman. The momentum of the impact carried the woman's body over the top of the hood of the car, her rear end thrust upward. Her long, flowing skirt flew over her head, revealing her muff, kitty, va-j-j, beef curtains, private parts or whatever you may call it. Unless they were invisible, her undergarments were AWOL (absent without leave). The scene of that accident became X-rated. Fortunately the woman walked away from the incident. The only thing seriously hurt was her pride.

The neighbor, curious to know why the woman jumped into the road, went to investigate and found a dead snake in the area in which she was walking.

Fear can cause us to do some senseless things. It is our choice to act in fear or to use what God has given us. ***Luke 10:19*** (NLV) says "Listen! I have given you power to walk on snakes. I have given you power over small animals with a sting of poison. I have given you power over all the power of the one works against you." Connecting this phrase: "God has given us love, power and a sound mind" with the scripture from Luke helps me to understand that God wants us to love ourselves enough that we will not put ourselves in harm's way. He has given us a sound mind to let us figure out what to do when we encounter danger. He has given us the power to overcome what works against us. God is greater than anything and everything. We do not have to be afraid. We can apply our faith to all that works against us because of God being in us. ***1 John 4:4*** says, "...greater is He that is in you, than he that is in the world." Being granted this powerful, effective life-changing word is like living with an awesome coach that stirs up our beastly potential to pulverize all the works against us.

Many people choose to live a life of isolation and loneliness because they are afraid of getting hurt. We must be aware that being hurt and disappointed by people can cause a subtle fear to take residence in us. In some cases, fear can infect the heart, immobilizing the flow of love in our lives like a deadly disease. Living without love is like not living at all. Despite the shield of armor we may use to guard our hearts, being hurt and disappointed are like Kryptonite to Superman. Somehow they still manage to get to us. Hurt and disappointed are facts of life. Those experiences build character and keep us balanced when we go through them correctly. Experiencing things that hurt us can also be humbling if we do not let pride consume us. Experiencing hurt reveals that we can be touched, and it can actually soften our hearts, preventing our hearts from turning to stone.

We all have done things to disappoint others. When it happens to us, we should be meek, merciful and forgiving. We think soundly when we remember that we too have been thoughtless, self-centered and inconsiderate concerning others at one time or another. We walk in love when we forgive and release our offenders. We experience the power that God has given us when we get over the offense quickly and let it go. Ultimately, we are free to laugh and enjoy the comedic encounters in life. Will Durst (a political comic) says, "Comedy is defiance. It's a snort of contempt in the face of fear and anxiety. And it's the laughter that allows hope to creep back on the inhale." Joy has no tolerance for the things that will keep us fearful. Joy sends disappointment and hurt feelings packing.

Without your permission, joy opens the door and invites hope to come in

The only type of fear that that I have found to be healthy is a respect and reverence for those things that are greater than us. God is greater. God's word is greater. Respecting the Lord, is the beginning of knowledge. ***(Proverbs 1:7)*** Someone once told me that "Knowledge is power." Putting into action the knowledge to do and say the right thing is powerful and can be profitable. Working in sales, I have found that quote to be true. When I would think the right thing, I would say the right thing and close the deal not being timid or insecure. ***Proverbs 18:21*** (KJV) says, "Death and life are in the power of the tongue: and they that love it shall eat the fruit thereof." God has given to us the creative power to speak life, health, wealth, joy and peace into our situations. We do not have to succumb to being overtaken by fear. Begin planting seeds of faith and have great expectations. Start speaking those things that be not as though they were, as mentioned in ***Romans 4:17,*** especially when challenging situations are knocking at your door. Dr. James taught me to confess, "I am the head and not the tail. I am going over and not under. I am above, not beneath. I have abundance and no lack." Confessions like this water desires planted in our hearts. Our expectations will align our thoughts and actions to receive.

The creative power of God's word takes more than just simply speaking in faith. We have to be patient. Some things take time. We must also demonstrate God's unconditional love for ourselves and others. Loving ourselves will give us a healthy outlook on being able to care for others regardless of their shortcomings. Loving people will activate God's blessings to come through people. Loving God, ourselves and others, pushes out the consuming effects of fear. ***I John 4:18*** says, "There is no fear in love; but perfect love casts out fear: because fear has torment. He that fear is not made perfect in love." Fear hinders love and is an enemy of joy.

The last of the trio is **lack of faith**. "...Whatsoever is not of faith is sin." ***Romans 14:23*** (KJV). When we do not have faith in God, we transgress against God. Unbeknownst to many, not having faith in God, we oppose ourselves. One day I was reading an article and it was about the awesome wonders of our planet Earth. It described the location of the Earth and how it is perfectly positioned in orbit in our solar system, in the region of the Milky Way galaxy. We are not too close to the center, and not too far from it. We are positioned about 93 million miles from the sun. This precise orbit is positioned within a zone that life neither freezes nor fries.

The article mentioned the function of the large, tailor made, illustrious moon. The diameter measures just over a quarter of the size of the earth, not like any other moon in the galaxy known. The moon is the principle cause of the ocean's tides which plays a vital role in Earth's ecology. The moon contributes to Earth's spin axis. Without the moon, our planet would wobble like a spinning top. Earth has a perfect tilt and spin. Its tilt is about 23.4 degrees, which causes the annual cycle of seasons. Scientists have discovered that if the earth, the sun and the moon were positioned any differently, it would be catastrophic.

The article explained how our planet is protected by an amazing armor. It has a dual protective shield, a magnetic field that is caused by the spinning ball of molten iron in the center of Earth, and a custom-made atmosphere, the ozone layer. The magnetic field protects us from cosmic radiation and deadly forces emanating from the sun. The ozone layer contains a form of oxygen which absorbs up to 99% of incoming ultraviolet radiation. The ozone layer helps protect us humans and the plankton we depend on to produce much of our oxygen.

After reading the article, I could only think of how precise and strategic God is. I felt compelled to praise God and marvel at his wonders. God's plan for our lives is just as precise as the creation of our planet. If He can tilt Earth precisely in a way that the seasons smoothly transition year after year, He can smoothly transition our lives during our seasons of trials and tribulations. If God has designed a magnetic field and an ozone layer to protect the human race, how much more believable is it that He has in motion a protective plan for our individual lives? Through the eyes of faith, we can see our salvation, our help, and our being rescued even before it happens.

There was a time when I experienced trials and I secretly disqualified God as being my protector. I felt like He was not there for me. At those times, I was only focusing on the few things that were bringing me trouble and not on the many fortunate things about my life. I am so very grateful that I am now in a different place. I have discovered that having faith in anything other than Him will set me on another course that will alter His precise strategic plan for my life. Everything that we say and do is based off of a belief system. Why not let our belief systems be in God? We all must humble ourselves and realize that the course that we devise will never measure up to our awesome Creator's.

As awesome and precise as God is, He created in every man a free will to choose. I can only imagine how God feels when we choose to believe in something else other than Him. ***Hebrews 11:6*** (KJV) says, "Without faith it is impossible to please Him." When God is not pleased because of our unbelief, it is tempting to think that He is ego tripping when we reap the consequences of our unbelief. However, He isn't ego tripping. He's not pleased because we hinder the laws that are set in motion for Him to bless us. Being a just, and loving God, everything about Him operates based off of His love and the laws that He has implemented. He has given all of us a fair shot to live by them. "God rewards them that diligently seek Him." ***(Hebrews 11:6)*** God is a God of order and principle. According to His law, He wants to rightfully and justly reward us. He is a God of sowing and reaping. If we sow faith, we reap blessings. The reward for having faith in God, is an emotional freedom of living a joyful life. ***Hebrews 11:1*** (KJV) says, "Faith is the substance of things hoped for, the evidence of things not seen."

Faith is an absolute which is exclusively the warranty of a believer

The price to pay for this warranty is humility. I love the fact that faith holds us in custody humbling us before our maker. While walking by faith, we must be void of arrogance and pride. We will have to allow the words of God to take the place of our thoughts. Faith will connect us to God being Lord over our thoughts, words and deeds. **Worrying**, **fear** and **lack of faith** are the subtle transgressions that we think are not so bad. Succumbing to them is not like frolicking in a field of pansies. But they are not fields of pansies; those fields are more like poison ivy. The results are just as damaging as an undetected, leaking pipe and as subtle as a drug addiction. They slowly and methodically do damage. We really need to see how they are agents that will cause us to decline joy. We must see that they will also remove us from the precise, strategic, glorious plan that God has already set in motion for our quality of living.

Growing up in the Ghetto, I have seen hard living because of **worry, fear** and **lacking faith** in God. I have seen Wisdom try to break through the generations of feeble thinking. However, from generation to generation, Wisdom would appear to be "Somewhere Over the Rainbow" with Dorothy and Toto. Poor choices would be made because of an ineffective belief system. We all believe in something. Instead of choosing the Wisdom of God, some of our belief systems would involve drunkenness, promiscuity, drugs, theft, gambling, and such like in an attempt to get some relief. ***Proverbs 1:7*** (KJV) says**,** "The fear of the Lord is the beginning of knowledge; but fools despise wisdom and instructions." Foolishness causes hardship. Wisdom empowers us not to get entrapped in **worry, fear** and **lacking faith** in God which alleviates us from unnecessary pain and suffering.

Despite the many harsh realities that I have experienced in my life, I have adopted a saying that I heard in an animated motion picture "Kung Fu Panda." The wise master was telling Panda that he was too concerned about what was and what will be. He went on to say, "The past is history, tomorrow is a mystery, but today is a gift. That is why we call it present." I believe that my every day is a present, a gift from God. Regardless of my circumstance, I live my today in the fullest. I make something good of my day every day on purpose. It is a gift. I take the time to savor the flavor of my gift. I inhale the essence of my gift. I allow my senses to be stimulated with the presence of my gift. Life's journey is so much better in the joy of the Lord.

Tribulation may sometimes feel like the Lord has abandoned us. We may feel that way, but He has not abandoned us. I personally know about battling with the feeling of abandonment. Going through this hardship, God instructed me to *Fear Not* and watch His salvation. I can happily say that as I journeyed through, God has never left me ashamed for trusting and believing in Him. This next story reveals how I got over the hurdle of feeling abandoned by people that meant the world to me and the feeling of being abandoned by God.

My family and I faithfully served in a ministry for twenty-four years, six days out of the week and sometimes seven. It was my dream to partner with my husband in ministry. We had the opportunity to relocate and start a church. We went through a major process before we branched off and was sent off with blessings. We were required to send money and our monthly reports to the church headquarters. Once we branched out, the church people who we served in ministry for all of those years quickly became cold and non-sociable. Their shift in attitude felt like our twenty-four years of service never existed. People were told not to talk to us and some hurtful things were said and done. The time that I thought would be one of the greatest times of my life, ended up being one of the greatest trials of my life.

My husband and I started our church. We had a nice little following. There was a woman in our church who was very needy and he and the woman became very friendly. My husband not being accountable to the word of God, began to alienate me as his relationship with this woman blossomed. As time progressed, their relationship went beyond that of a pastor-and-member relationship. They literally did almost everything together alone. He refused to stop despite how I felt about it. Over time, he grew weary of me confronting him about his behavior and invited me to leave our church first and then eventually our home. His actions caused me to feel like I was discarded like a disposable diaper instead of being treasured as how a wife should be treated, "... worth far more than rubies...." ***Proverbs 31:10***

It was a very painful moment in my life. I went from being a licensed and ordained pastor with many accomplishments over a span of twenty-four years to being homeless, carless, friendless . . . and now husband-less . . . after knowing him for twenty-eight years. Living in a new land, I had to start over with just about everything. I found a place near my job and for ten months, I walked to work and walked miles to the grocery store. I dodged cars and trucks in areas that there were no sidewalks. A truck actually came so close that it grazed my leg. The driver saw that he hit me when my cart on wheels flung away from me. He stopped, apologized and stated that he did not see me. Sunshine or rain, I had to walk on back country roads in the south. After building up my beautiful home over the past twenty-four years of my life, I was left with little to nothing to start my life all over again. I slept on the floor with pillows and then an air mattress for six months. For ten months, I sat on the floor in my living room until I was able to get furniture.

In the midst of this trial, the Lord led me to go to Pastor Robyn Gool's Sunday morning service. He took us to ***I Peter 5:7*** (KJV) which says, "Cast all your care upon the Lord for He cares for you." He then gave the J. B. Phillips translation (NTV) that says "You can throw the whole weight of your anxieties upon Him for you are His personal concern." I was touched deeply while he ministered. I desperately needed to be reminded that I was the Lord's personal concern. I no longer had the care and support of my pastors, church family or husband. Not having a support group, I was in a survival mode and emotionally numb. Two of the most meaningful relationships in my life existed no longer and I could not understand why God had allowed such a thing despite all of my praying and seeking Him. I had to get over the hurtle of abandonment that could have easily caused me to worry, be fearful and lack faith in God.

I thank God for Pastor Robyn Gool and the other TV ministers such as Joyce Myers, Joel Osteen, TD Jakes, Betty and James Robinson and Creflo Dollar. I had a morning and evening feast of them which kept me encouraged. I am so glad that I took heed to the gold nuggets of God's wisdom and revelations to get me through this major transition in my life. He covered, protected and loved on me. God put a mandate on the inside of me not to worry, fret, or be afraid, because He was with me. I am now happier than I have ever been in my entire life. God has restored and increased my blessings. My home is beautiful even more than before. I have a very nice vehicle even nicer than before. I live more financially comfortable than before. I attend a terrific church. I am also blessed to have family and friends who celebrate and appreciate me. But most importantly, God is with me and the peace and joy that I now experience is priceless.

I am happy to say my heart is clean and free of those negative emotions that are no substitute for a quality life. Negative emotions will damper any new relationship that we may attempt to form. I have been victimized, but I am not a victim. I choose not to be. I have experienced some really harsh realities in my life. However, I am "more than a conqueror" ***(Romans 8:37)***. God knew what I was going to go through, when I was going to go through, and how I was going to go through. ***Urban Joy*** would not be written if I did not go through these things. So many people have been helped as a result of my experiences. God's plan for my life is just as precise as the creation of planet Earth. God's plan is never selfish. It is not just for one or a few, it is for all. The things that we go through ultimately are to make us better and to help someone else. I have stepped into my true purpose for living. If you are one to say, *Life is hard and that is why I can't be joy*, there is light at the end of the tunnel. Trust God with all your heart and rejoice over His precise plan for your life. Life will not be hard even while going through hardship. I can testify that you will be so much happier.

Know that every day is a good day regardless of the rain, pain, and strain of hardships.

If you are one to say, **(3) "Joy is an emotion that erupts only when good things happen ,"** let's see what God's word says about it. ***James 1:2*** (KJV) says, "Count it all joy when you fall into diverse temptations." God's word is saying be joyful even when good things are not happening. I have heard many expound on this verse of scripture before I got the true meaning of it. I would think to myself, "Okay, I have to put a smile on my face" even while still perplexed with not knowing what to do with my bad feelings. I even literally thought to numerically count, "one joy, two joy, three joy, four joy" like counting sheep with hopes that joy would overtake me. My understanding had not even scratch the surface of the revelation of this scripture. Experiencing hardship, God helped me to understand how I can count it all joy.

Feeling pain is an indication that our nervous system is functioning properly. It is natural to want to react when we feel pain. It is natural to react when we feel the sting of adversity. The Lord revealed to me that we spiritually function properly when we count it all joy during times that tempts us not to be joyful. The word *count* means to *consider* in the context of James 1:2. God's word does not say, *"feel through it* with all joy." It says, *"Count it* all joy." We literally can consider joy when experiencing adversity. Instead of saying foul, ungodly things, devising all sorts of plans to bring vengeance, or whatever else we might do when we spiral down into being negative, we can put on the brakes, breathe and consider joy. I can attest to countless times I would stop and say to myself, "Is this matter worth declining my joy, acting like a fool or giving up the quality of my day? My answer would *always* be, "No!" I would shake myself and enjoy the rest of my day.

Reacting with negative feelings can be counterproductive in

successfully handling adversities. We shouldn't put too much into our feelings. Our feelings have proven to be wrong, unstable, unpredictable, hormonal, and have lead us in the wrong direction. Joy is stable, predictable, trustworthy and is proven to be productive. The joy of the Lord goes beyond a feeling. Joy is always present in us and full of power (as God is) even if we do not feel joy. Faith in God keeps us from declining in our ever-present joy.

Our faith gives us the unction to tap into our joy that is immediate, just waiting to be jump-started

It is possible to experience joy while going through painful experiences. Until I experienced it, I would have never thought that being joy was even possible while experiencing excruciating pain. This next story proved me wrong:

One morning I started my morning regimen by walking. After my walk, I returned home to get ready for work. I started to experience pain in my right side that progressed from bad to worse. Once I hit the floor in pain, I called my doctor. The doctor on staff told me that I should go to Urgent Care. I then called my adopted daughter Lydia who lived nearby. Lydia arrived quickly and drove me to Urgent Care. I must tell you, there is nothing urgent at Urgent Care. If your number is twenty, regardless of your pain and suffering, you have to wait until your number is called. Having only one doctor on call makes it worse. Referring to a pain chart, my pain fluctuated from eight to ten. I could not sit in the waiting room. I tried standing and leaning on the wall but it was insufferable. I decided to lie down and moan and groan in my car. When the medical team was ready to escort me to the examination room, Lydia came for me. In the examination room, I still waited so long that the nurse stuck her head in, apologized and said that it would probably be thirty minutes more. The doctor came in well beyond that thirty-minute estimate to examine me. After the examination, he concluded that I needed to go to the Emergency Room. His concern was that the area in pain could be my appendix or ovaries. Unfortunately, they did not have the equipment to do an ultrasound.

Altogether, I was there for three hours only to be told that I needed to go to the ER. OMG (Oh My Goodness!), my emergency was nothing immediate there either. I lay across a chair for another hour and a half before they called me in the back to be examined. Shortly after I arrived at the emergency ward, my daughter Angie and her husband Kris arrived. When I saw little mother's (Angie's) face I was so happy I shed a little tear. During that 90-minute wait, they all told funny stories, and I laughed nonstop. *I laughed right in the midst of the pain.* I remember holding myself trying to laugh while at the same time trying to avoid myself more pain. It felt weird to laugh while being in that much pain. I was concerned that if the hospital staff saw me laughing it would prolong my wait to be examined. I tried to laugh discretely but they wouldn't stop telling funny stories . . . and I didn't stop laughing.

Joy, is it to be or not to be? That was the question that day in the Emergency Ward. I was tempted to complain that something was always going wrong. I could have continued to wallow in my pain. I could have murmured and complained about the looooonnng wait. In doing so, I would have made my situation worse. ***I Corinthians 10:10*** says, "Neither murmur ye, as some of them also murmured, and were destroyed of the destroyer." Instead, when the opportunity presented itself, I gladly took the opportunity to laugh.

I was finally called back to be examined. They checked my vitals, pumped me up with pain medicine. After they had examined me, I was glad that I did not release the destroyer because the examination revealed that I had a large dermoid cyst on my ovaries. A dermoid cyst is dense and originates from a stem cell that develops skin tissue, teeth and hair. It sounded like a little monster was growing on my ovaries. They scheduled an emergency appointment for me to see a physician within that week. During my follow-up visit with the doctor, she informed me that it is common for a cyst that heavy to twist the ovary, causing severe pain and then twist back. She told me that I was within four centimeters of being in danger of losing my life and she was going to schedule surgery the following month to remove the ovary. She stated that if I felt pain prior to our scheduled appointment, get immediate attention. I asked the doctor what is the possibility of it going away just like it came? She said it was highly unlikely. I did not want face surgery again. I did not want to lose my ovary. So my prayer partners and I had a month to pray that cyst away to prevent surgery. My co-worker Casey shared with me that during her clinical training, she learned about the cyst and the type of damage it could do to one's body. She also learned that if the cyst goes untreated it could cause death. Working in the hospital, she became aware of the cyst causing death to some people. After being examined, the doctor told me to take it easy and rest more. That is exactly what I did as well as confessed that the cyst would dissolve.

About three weeks later, my daughter Angie did her usual checking on her momma. She asked me how I felt and if I still felt something in the affected area. I told her from time to time I would feel a sharp pain on my side but then it would go away. After I said that, she got silent. Then she sounded like she was crying. With a choked up voice, she started apologizing repeatedly, saying, "I am sorry, Mom. I'm so sorry." To my surprise, my daughter was laughing! She was laughing profusely! When she finally composed herself, she told me that when I told her I get a sharp pain from time to time, with her animated mind she pictured the cyst having jacked-up teeth under a thick mustache biting my side. I hollered. I saw a vivid picture of that in my mind and laughed to tears for about a good ten minutes straight. That was some good medicine.

During my follow up visit, the doctor reported that the dermoid had shrunk to half its size, something she had never seen happen with any of her patients during her career. She said that she had always scheduled surgery during the follow-up visit, but she scheduled me to come back in two months. Two months later, the examination was extensive. The ultrasound technician probed me until it was very uncomfortable. It seemed as if what she was looking for could not be found. I asked her, "Should the examination hurt like this? Do you see anything?" She politely said, "The doctor will talk with you concerning the results of the examination." When the doctor came into the room I could not wait to hear what she had to say. After reading the report, the doctor rolled her chair around to face me and said, "It looks like you don't have a dermoid. Your ovaries are perfectly fine." Right there, on the examination table, **I praised God**!

"A merry heart does good like a medicine." (***Proverbs 17:22)*** I whole heartedly believe this scripture. I believe choosing to laugh throughout my situation helped the process of my healing. A cyst growing on my ovaries, threatening my life, was not a good thing. The temptation to worry, complain, feel sorry for myself, act mean or defensive, be angry with God, etc., was there. But I chose to count it all as joy. I considered joy while in pain. During those challenging times I chose to laugh and absorb all the joy around me (my Joy AC Adapters). My joy helped me to be sober and positively productive as the Lord helped me through that adverse time

Philippians 4:4 (KJV) says, "Rejoice in the Lord always and again I say rejoice." Apostle Paul was exhorting the Christians in Philippi. He was very much aware of their labor, trials and persecution as he experienced the same. Yet, his message to the believers is "Always rejoice." Many times, we have done the opposite when faced with adversity. To me, Philippians 4:4 sounds like a call to *check yourself and snap to it* scripture when hit with adversity. It is the type of scripture that God cares enough to prepare us for when adversity will hit us over and over again. God's solution is to be joyful in Him over and over again. It doesn't give us the space for the mediocre level of making excuses. When Apostle Paul wrote to the believers in Thessalonica, he told them something very similar: "Rejoice ever more." ***(I Thessalonians 5:16).*** The definition of *rejoice* is "to be joyful" and ever more means "forever." It is absolutely wonderful to serve a God that wants us to be *joy* (great happiness; delight; a source of happiness undoubted) forever. This is an awesome divine privilege that God has given to every one of us. The only thing we have to do is believe it and cooperate with it. A fact that motivates me to consistently be joy is to remember that my life will spiral down without it. I will not live a quality life without being joy.

God's word is like an anchor and will help us stay grounded. If the word of God is not our focal point, we will drift away from being joy. God had to raise the bar for us to always rejoice because there is always something lurking to try our patience. There is always something ever present that can frustrate us. Disappointment can play Russian roulette with our emotions daily. It is natural for us to react to the things that affect us negatively. However, our belief and discipline aids us in being joy consistently. God would not tell us to rejoice evermore if it was not possible. If God gave us an inch of permission to act out, by us being human, that inch of permission would be one of our favorite scriptures. God does not have to tell us to rejoice ever more when things are going great. It is natural for us to do that. He is telling us to rejoice when things aren't going so great. We have to depend upon the supernatural, to be resilient. ***Urban Joy*** enables us to bounce ourselves right into rejoicing ever more, in spite of our circumstances. No longer taking pleasure in acting out, will also put us on the right path.

There was a season in my life in which I lost just about everything:

most of my possessions, family, marriage, ministry status and people I thought were my friends. The things that happened to me were not good. I honestly did not feel joy. There was nothing apparent to count as joy, let alone all joy. However, every day was a new day and every day by faith I found a way to consider joy. Every day I found a reason to smile. Every day I looked for something to laugh about on purpose. Every day I found a way to be grateful for all that I had. I experienced the power of joy, the present tense of ***Urban Joy*** -- and it didn't cost me a thing. I refused to trust my feelings or to cooperate with them. I knew if I did that for a minute, my feelings would take me down like a four-hundred-pound linebacker sacking a one-hundred-pound punter.

I Peter 1:6 encourages us to "rejoice while in our seasons of heaviness through manifold temptations." There will be seasons in our life that we will have many various things to have to overcome. Seasons in our life that impatience will strongly tempt us to turn away from the ways of God. Stay strong because the outcome of our faith being tried will prove to be more precious than gold ***(I Peter 1:7)*** Our faith is going to be tried. We can "rejoice with joy unspeakable full of His glory" that is mentioned in ***I Peter 1:8*** because we belong to Him. Rejoicing with joy unspeakable full of His glory is our inheritance. We are richly blessed because we belong to Him.

Revelations 22:13 (KJV) God says, "I am the Alpha and Omega the beginning and the end, the first and the last." With God being my Father, I live with the reality that the beginning and the end of my life is secure in Him. I have won every battle even before the battle has begun. I have overcome every adversity even before day one. My heavenly Father is the first and last of my life. He has the final say. Truly understanding this fact, should put a smile on every believer's face. It changes how I see everything. Nothing else matters.

Adversities will always challenge us with the question, "Joy, is it to be or not to be?" When Wisdom speaks, the answer is always:

"To Be Joy"

~Misconceptions about Joy~

The older I get, the more I have witnessed and personally experienced innumerable misconceptions and false impressions about various things. The online *Free Dictionary by Farlex* defines *misconception* as "a mistaken idea or view, resulting from a misunderstanding." Synonyms are: fallacy, delusion, misapprehension, misconstruction, mistaken belief, false impression, misunderstanding, misreading, and error. The following short story was retold to me by someone whose family member, a distributor, had related to him. The story is about a gentleman whose misconception left a drastic, unforgettable impression. Naturally if we keep living, we will get older and our bodies will change.

The gentleman in the story was getting up there in age. To his lament, he experienced what is common with some men: a particular body part was malfunctioning. He decided to try a drug called Viagra. He did not know how to administer the drug, so he asked a relative. The relative, who had a *mistaken idea,* a *misreading,* and was certainly in error on how to administer the drug, *told him to chew it*! When the drug started to take effect, it missed its target. Instead, stiff as a board, his tongue protruded out of his mouth. He could not tuck it, hide it or control it. His tongue was so stiff that he felt the strain all the way to the back of his neck. Seeing no other option, he called 911. Can you imagine what that call sounded like to the dispatcher? I have heard many sermons about bridling our tongues but this method wins the gold. I tell this story in light humor; however, we should read the warning labels and consult our physicians when taking any drug.

This story reinforces the significance of making sure we get the facts and obtain full understanding before we conclude on any matter. To avoid believing a misconception, even when we think we have the facts, we still should not be hasty in our conclusions. We should always look for the best solution in any situation. The best solution may not always be the popular choice, it may not be the quickest answer, and it may take more effort and time that we are willing to give. But at the end of the day, we will be most satisfied not having to invest more time correcting mistakes and errors.

The subject of joy is no exception. If we want to live a joyful life, we must learn the facts about joy.

It is a misconception that consistently being joy means that we are going to be silly, giddy and laughing every minute of the day

Consistently being joy does not equate to wearing a senseless grin at all times. Joy is an inward posture that flows outward. Being joy expresses a sense of being light-hearted. Formulating a painted smile doesn't depict authentic joy. Joy is a current that flows through our thoughts, our body language, our words. Being joy will manifest a smile, a smile that is the result of an infusion of God's Spirit with our spirits. God created us to infuse His spirit with ours. The day it becomes our priority is the day we will experience the bliss of heaven.

The *Bible* refers to *joy* as *being of the Lord.* ***(Nehemiah 8:10)*** The Lord is our source and He wants to ignite us. We are privileged to be blessed with the joy of the Lord. It does not matter where we are or in what situation we find ourselves, the Lord is ever-present. He promises that "He will never leave us nor forsake us."***(Hebrews 13:5)*** Being ever-present, we can always draw from Him. We can always be blessed with the privilege of joy. I have been walking with Christ for more than thirty years and have seen the times when we as believers forget to draw from His presence. When we forget, we often respond negatively to adversity. It is indisputable that to be good is upright. If we want to house joy consistently, then responding uprightly is the thing to do. God promises in ***Psalms 84:11***(KJV), "No good thing will He withhold from them that walk uprightly." To *walk upright* is to *behave in a positive, moral and or honorable manner*. When we behave uprightly, joy and many other great things are promised by God. In ***Ecclesiastes 2:26*** (KJV), God promises to give a man that is good in his sight, wisdom, knowledge and **joy**. We all know that to be good can be a struggle at times. When we are wronged, even if we are strong in our convictions, we are compelled to respond with vengeance or something questionable that may bring us temporary satisfaction.

The satisfaction is temporary because God has given to every man a conscience. The Lord gave us a conscience to know the difference between right and wrong. When we behave wrongly, our consciences will bother us. A troubled conscience hinders the flow of joy and it clutters our minds which could also hinder us in making the wisest decisions. For any of this to matter, we have to be weary of living a life of being partially fulfilled. Many people may pride themselves in being happy without the Lord. However, the fullness of joy as mentioned in the scriptures will only be experienced through Him. I challenge anyone and everyone living a partially fulfilled life to see what it feels like to experience the fullness of joy. I also double-dog dare anyone and everyone who think they are experiencing the fullness of joy to live ***Urban Joy***. I can guarantee that you will like the fullness of ***Urban Joy*** better.

***It is a misconception that being joy all the time excludes being* serious**

One of the definitions of *serious* is *to be sober.* ***I Peter 1:13*** exhorts us to *gird up the loins of our mind, and to be sober.* Being joy is being sober minded. You are sober when you assess a situation and seriously choose not to be negative but choose to be joyful. Not being joy is not being sober. Not being joy is actually being foolish. The *Webster's II New Riverside University Dictionary* defines *foolish* as *unwise; lacking good sense or judgment.* Good judgment would cause one to want to draw from wisdom. God's wisdom instructs us to be joyful always. Every day I see people repel wisdom and carry out handling matters negatively. ***Proverbs 1:7*** says, "... but fools despise wisdom and instruction." Fools do not choose to handle life in joy. ***Proverbs 19:10*** (KJV) says, "Delight is not seemly for a fool." *Delight* means *great joy* or *pleasure*. Always being annoyed is foolish. ***Proverbs 12:16*** (NIV) says, "Fools show their annoyance at once, but the prudent overlook an insult." If we find that we are always annoyed and or offended, we need to put ourselves in check with the word of God and change only if our peace matters. "Great peace have they which love thy law: and nothing shall offend them." ***Psalm 119:165*** (KJV)

I personally know the effects of being a fool by showing my annoyance. I remember the times when I came through like the Looney Tunes Tasmanian devil. I had to clean up the debris and social casualties as a result of my behavior. When I got angry I kicked holes in doors, threw things and yelled like a "bat out of hell." I was very young and immature. However, one day the Lord dealt with my heart severely. He put me on a study concerning anger. I studied for a year about the wrath of man, anger, and being slow to speak. I now have a conviction concerning acting foolish and will no longer freely act annoyed. The following three scriptures in the King James Version helped me to steer away from always acting out of annoyance and offense:

1. ***James 1:20*** (KJV) "For the wrath of man worketh not the righteousness of God."
2. ***James 1:19*** (KJV), "Wherefore, my beloved brethren, let every man be swift to hear, slow to speak, slow to wrath."
3. ***Proverbs 15:1*** (KJV), "A soft answer turneth away wrath: but grievous words stir up anger."

At this point in my life, I may confront with the heart of getting an understanding and to dissolve a misunderstanding. However, being foolish is no longer my choice.

As believers, we should never find ourselves in the position of being fools. ***Psalms 14:1***(KJV) says "The fool has said in his heart there is no God." If we choose to handle a matter foolishly, God is absent from that situation. Like fools, our actions are mocking, "There is no God." The Wisdom from above will help us to distinguish the difference between being serious and being foolish. Joy is an expression of sobriety coupled with God's wisdom and knowledge about how He wants us to conduct ourselves.

It is a misconception that joy is obtained by way of possessions

Many believe that having money is the missing element that will bring them joy, but this is not a prerequisite for the joy of living. In the pursuit of happiness, man strives to obtain things. Some of us get a huge house, shop until we drop, have wild sex, take drugs, get married impulsively, collect things, and so on searching for happiness. I personally know millionaires that still live good portions of their lives unhappy. Joy clearly has nothing to do with having money or possessions. Obtaining wealth and money should not be our first priority. ***Matthew 6:33*** Jesus has set the order of what our priority should be, "But seek ye first the kingdom of God, and his righteousness; and all other things shall be added unto you."

Generally when God's kingdom (righteousness, peace and joy) is not the first priority being sought, there exists a void of never having enough and never being content. God's Kingdom is everlasting, and it fulfills every void. It is humanistic to obtain things that yield a temporary moment of joy and a brief illusion of contentment.

Humanistic joy is like visiting a Joy "Rent-a-Center" while failing to claim the "down-to-the-core" joy of the Lord

To experience the depth of joy that we need to live a quality life, we should take heed to the guidance of the creator of joy. Joy *from* God equals fellowship *with* God. Fellowshipping with God is simply talking to God and positioning ourselves to allow Him to talk back. King David said in ***Psalms 34:4*** (KJV) "I sought the Lord and He answered me." King David also said in ***Psalms 34:15*** (KJV) "The eyes of the Lord are upon the righteous and His ears are attentive to their cry." God talks to us through His word. He will give us a personal, tailor-made word that is always in conjunction with His Holy scriptures. While in fellowship with God, let Him tell you what He wants from you. He always has a listening ear to hear what you have to say to Him. When we connect with God, our lives are more meaningful and beautiful. They become positively delightful.

One of my favorite scriptures is ***Psalms 37:4*** (KJV) "Delight yourself in the Lord and He will give you the desires of your heart." There is nothing wrong with being blessed with many things, but possessing things, great or small, means nothing without true joy. If you are wealthy but an emptiness still resides within you, let the joy of the Lord fill the void. Materialistic gains are lifeless until the joy of the Lord brings everything to life.

On another note, for more than thirty years I have seen Christians go sideways by heavily focusing on things being added to them. They believe that they are *seeking God's kingdom first* because they are in church doing it. They get off balance by intensely stuffing themselves on prosperity teachings. Their motive for giving is to receive, receive, and receive. They speak much about obtaining the latest technology, getting the finest cars, mansions, and wearing designer clothes and jewelry. They don't see the lost. They conjure up many projects and events not really helping anyone. They are blinded by their desire to prosper and can't see the people that need help right in front of them.

Sadly, I have seen many prosperity seekers fizzle out of ministry gravely disappointed and unfulfilled.

I have also seen many go sideways who are just functioning in the church. They are not "seeking first the kingdom of God" or fulfilling the purpose for the kingdom. They believe that they are doing so because they serve on committees raising money, but what they are really doing is working feverishly to build a man's kingdom. Most of the money doesn't go to the community. It doesn't go to the lost. It goes to making their leaders look good. Consequently, they live very unfulfilled, dissatisfied lives in many ways. They believe or are being told by their leaders that one day their ships of blessings will come in for their hard work in ministry. Yet while waiting and working, they watch their leaders' ships come in year after year, fulfilling their purposes and pockets. We all have a purpose given by God in this life.

Fulfilling your divine purpose yields a depth of joy that cannot be substituted

If you are unhappy, you may not have tapped into your purpose for the kingdom. I am a witness; living your kingdom's purpose will manifest "all other things being added unto you" as stated in ***Matthew 6:33***.

God is a just God. ***Numbers 23:1*** (KJV) says, "God is not a man, that he should lie; neither the son of man, that he should repent: hath he said, and shall he not do it? or hath he spoken, and shall he not make it good?" He is not going to have you working like a Hebrew slave without due payment. God is not going to have us feverishly working for His kingdom and not fulfill His promises. ***Luke 10:7*** (KJV) says, "A laborer is worthy of his hire." God considers us worthy of being blessed with abundance coupled with spiritual contentment of peace and joy. Every area of your life is important to your heavenly Father.

If you are working and working and working in a ministry and are not prospering, you need to seek God to see what principles are being violated. You need to identify what is robbing you of an abundant life. Christ says, "The thief cometh not, but for to steal, and to kill, and to destroy: I am come that they might have life, and that they might have it more abundantly." ***John 10:10*** (KJV) *Abundantly* means *in large quantities, occurring in or marked by abundance; plentiful*. If you are working with all your heart in ministry and are not experiencing an abundant life, something is wrong. If you are always borrowing and begging, struggling week after week, month after month, and year after year, something is wrong. It doesn't line up with God's word.

In God's kingdom, we are the chosen helping the needy, not the needy chosen to be helped

Even when working in ministry with all your heart and soul, there are seasons that God will try your faith. However, your entire journey with the Lord should not be trying. If you are struggling ten, twenty, thirty years living under the poverty level, something is wrong. If your church is struggling ten, twenty, thirty years to grow, pay the bills and staff and keeping up with the maintenance of the building, something is wrong. He is a rewarding God who promises and blesses. God cannot lie. Billy Graham, Bishop Bill Hamon, TD Jakes, Joyce Myers and so many more are great examples of men and women of God who are doing their divine purpose. They started with pretty much nothing and now they have a want for nothing. They are helping their loved ones, people in their community and all over the world. I have tapped into my divine purpose. I have worked full-time ministry, but I did not stop there. I sought the Lord first concerning my divine purpose. He has me on course and I have never been to this level of joy and blessings in my entire life. God has graced me to do it and I am a blessing to my family, church, community and the world.

In essence, doing great deeds for men or organizations will not render joy as we might suppose. Seeking first God's kingdom will put you on course with your divine purpose and joy with depth will permeate the core of your being. **Pray** and *ask God to show you* how to seek His Kingdom first and put you on course with your divine purpose for living. Your whole life will not be just consumed with working in an organization not flourishing; you will not be consumed with fulfilling your leaders' purposes and pockets. You will be a blessing to your loved ones, church, community and the world.

It is a misconception that people need to depend on others to be joy

This misconception is tough to recognize because we are raised to depend on our parents or guardians. A great portion of our lives consists of being totally dependent upon others for everything. When we become adults, we must develop the ability to function on our own. However, it takes many events, circumstances and much trial and error to learn. Even as adults some of us have still not quite learned. We still have a dysfunctional need for others. Some of us fantasize about depending on people with the perfect picture in our mind that those individuals would make us happy. Having people in our lives can be healthy, wonderful, and we will experience joyous moments with them. However, Wisdom will never direct us to depend on people to make us happy.

I remember making that mistake, especially during my birthday. When I was still married to my ex, I asked him to throw me a party for my fortieth birthday. Oh how I fantasized on how people were going to celebrate me, and that I was going to be so happy. I imagined that he would probably rent a place and have all of my loved ones come and celebrate this milestone event. I imagined that the celebration of me would stimulate the joy of turning forty. This was the first time in the twenty years of our marriage that I asked for a party, so I thought that my request was not unreasonable. In my mind, this birthday was going to be the crescendo of all birthdays. It was going to help make the transition of me growing old in grace just lovely. Sadly, I would have to say that birthday was the worst. I did not depend on God to be joyful about turning forty. I totally depended on people.

Every Sunday, nine of us always had dinner at a family member's home. My husband decided to acknowledge my birthday there. We did the norm; we were not at a hall or ballroom as I had pictured; we were in a small two-bedroom apartment. He went to the grocery store after church and bought me a birthday cake and had the bakery inscribe it to say Happy Birthday to me and an 18-year-old. I had to share my fortieth birthday with an 18-year-old! He liked her and deemed it important to put her name on my cake. He thought it would be a wonderful idea. I thought, "What kind of stuff is that? Was this supposed to make me feel better about turning forty?" It was obvious he had not made any previous arrangements. All of his efforts were done on the fly within a span of one hour. I was given two choice cards from the dollar store and a big fat box of nothing wrapped in, "Sorry, Babe, can't do *nothin'* else for ya."

Needless to say, I was stunned. I went speechless and numb when they unveiled the cake. I was deeply offended. I could not believe that he was unwilling to at least put forth a genuine effort in making this birthday special for me. My face must have revealed my disappointment because a couple of people there asked me was I feeling okay. All I could do was nod. He was blindly insensitive to my feelings. Over the decades of years together, "I would celebrate his stinkin' birthday," I thought to myself. I went out of my way to make it special for him. I could not understand, why this one time, he could not return the effort and consideration. At that time, I did not have the revelation of ***Urban Joy***. It took me about a year before I dropped the offense.

His actions didn't help much. I could not get over the fact that he felt so close to this 18-year-old that he thought her birthday should have been celebrated with mine. Strangely, he took her on a movie date right after this event. Putting more salt to the wound, they did it without me knowing. I found out a couple of weeks later. I questioned why he, a married man, thought that his actions were okay. He casually brushed it off by saying that it was for her birthday. I shared with him that we do things like that as a family. He stated that he wanted to take her, not us as a family. I had no idea that they were that close.

A few months later, I was still trying to swallow how insensitive he was concerning my birthday. Unfortunately, another incident occurred regarding another young woman and the subject of birthdays. Riding home that day, my husband shared with me and my daughter that he was going to buy a young lady, one whom I agreed to take into my home to groom like my own daughter, a television for her birthday. (My ex and this young woman, against my better judgment, became very chummy over the years while she lived there and they developed their own personal relationship. They played basketball together, went to the store, watched movies and so on, all without the girls and me.) When I asked why he was buying her such an expensive gift, he said, "I think she deserves it." That was the moment that I blew that car up like a mad black-woman terrorist. Reflecting as far back as I could, she was not cooking, cleaning, washing his clothes, feeding him in bed, taking good care of him, helping him in whatever he needed, bearing his children and taking good care of them! Thus, him saying that she deserved it, equated to him saying that the $15.00 cake and two fifty-cent cards were what I deserved. I also thought, "What did she do to deserve a television?"

I learned from these moments not to fantasize on what people could do to make me happy. Those experiences were likened to a splash of cold water in my face, a wake up and smell the coffee, or a brisk slap that made me say, "Thanks, I needed that." I was reminded that we as people can be self-absorbed, temperamental, and less than considerate. People forget and or do not value or appreciate all that we do for them. I have come to a conclusion that being human, we are limited, we make mistakes and we are not consistent in showing appreciation.

There is hope in all of this. The hope is that God is consistent. God is perfect. God does not make mistakes, and He loves us unconditionally. He will bless us even if we do not deserve it. (***Matthew 5:45***) Instead of fantasizing on what people could do to make me happy, I now focus on fulfilling my purpose and pursuing my dreams. We will maintain our joy by meditating on the things in which God takes pleasure. God takes pleasure in us fulfilling our destines. I have learned not to participate much with things that will not reap benefits. I pretty much do not involve my emotions or time if I am not certain that it is worth it. I spend much time with being in relationship with God because he is fool-proof. One thing I know for certain, if God promises, God will deliver. ***2 Corinthians 1:20*** (KJV) "For all the promises of God in him are yea (yes), and in him Amen (so be it)…" If I had the revelation of ***Urban Joy*** before that event, I know I would have handled it so much better. I wouldn't have declined joy. I probably would have had a clear view of reality. The reality was, my ex had another agenda. I would have seen the signs that his interest, focus and attention was not in pleasing me. Seeing clearly, I probably would have figured out some way to celebrate myself. If there are people in your life that will celebrate you, that is wonderful! but if not, ***Urban Joy*** will activate you to *like* yourself, *love* yourself, *enjoy* yourself and *celebrate* yourself.

Another example of an unhealthy dependency upon people: I have heard many parents say that their children are their reasons for living; their children are their happiness. I must tell you that depending upon your children to be your reason for living and happiness is like a plane crash waiting to happen. It is dysfunctional. It imposes unfair expectations on the children. Having children can be a joy, but our children are lent to us to manage and to help to shape them into being productive members of society. We are to pass down the wholesome traditions of our family and faith. While raising our children, our goal should be to eliminate our dysfunctions, allowing our children to have a much better life than we did. Our children are not given to us for us to own or to live our lives through them. We have our own divine purpose; so do they. As parents, we should be in a place to help and mold them to seek God in that manner. As parents, it is our job not to pass down our dysfunctions to our children. It is dysfunctional to put the burden of responsibility on our children to ensure our success or happiness.

Our foundation of happiness should be internal from an eternal source and not from an external source

It is healthy for our children to grow up and have lives of their own. It is healthy for them not to include or involve us in everything they do. Children appreciate seeing that their parents are happy with lives of their own. Our children will be strained and stressed if they feel responsible for our happiness. Children are not graced for such a task. If you love your children, allow joy to flow through your very existence in everything that you do. Always be that source of strength and joy that they can depend on, even in maturity. As parents we are equipped and graced for this task. Someone told me a tragic story of a father seeing his son die in his arms at the scene of a car accident because of a negligent drunken driver. He had other children and a wife. Of course, the event put a strain on the entire family, but as the years progressed, the father is still grieving, the mother has become an alcoholic and the other children are left with both the tragic death of their brother and the tragic loss of their parents. The lives of the parents died with the son. They declined the joy of living. The love for their other children was not enough to pull out of the grief. The Lord has graced us as parents to handle hardship, but it is only through Him. If we turn our backs on God and choose to be angry, we are hurting ourselves and the others around us who so desperately need us. Children are lent to us. Some of us have more time with our children than others. Death is a harsh reality. We do not get to choose the amount of time that we get to be with our loved ones. Before that time expires, we should live it up with them in joy, striving never to regret a lost moment. I lost my first grand baby. I had little time to enjoy him. He is with the Lord. I enjoyed Elijah growing in my daughter's stomach. I enjoyed watching him kick and punch her belly. I celebrated the idea of him with Little Mother (Angie). I held his little body when he was born and rubbed his little cheeks. He was beautiful. I do not regret one lost moment with my grandson Elijah.

Another harmful act of dependency that I have experienced and witnessed is improper dependency on pastors. This unhealthy dependency fixates on the idea of a pastor serving up happiness on a platter. There was a time I thought, "All I have to do is talk to my pastor about my situation and he is going to, like magic, make my problems go away." Pastors are not magicians. They are not going to put all of our unhappiness in a bag and say, "Abracadabra!" and *poof* our unhappiness disappears. A pastor's job is to direct us to the word of God for our everyday living. Pastors are to direct us to reroute our thinking to successfully count our diversities all joy. They should clearly through the word of God, help us get back on track in order to make the right decisions. If your pastor does anything other than that, that should be a cause for concern.

Improper dependency on a pastor can be the breeding ground for unsavory relationships. If a pastor comforts and strokes in a way that does not encourage godly moral principles, God is not in it. God will never lead us contrary to His word just so that we can be appeased in some physical way. Pastors are not doctors making house calls, massage therapists, sex therapists, boyfriends/girlfriends and or shower buddies to anyone other than their spouses. Pastors are called by God to be His messengers. They are the mouthpieces of God. They are called to watch over our souls and not our bodies. They are the watchmen that are to protect us from wandering away from God's fold. We must be careful about falling into a "Hero Syndrome" (strong displaced feelings for our rescuer). To conclude on the subject of depending on pastors, God is our eternal hero whose ulterior motive is unconditional love. God's word guides us away from depending on the arm of man. He instructs us to respect His servants, but He wants us to totally depend on Him.

The misconception of depending on people for joy can be summed up in a few words. We must void ourselves of that type dependency. It is good to have people in our lives who support, love and cherish us. But all people will not always support, love and cherish us. If we find ourselves without, let us be reminded of the inspired words of King David in ***Psalms 42:5.*** The enemy raided his camp, causing him to lose everything. If that wasn't enough, all of the men that he supported and covered in battle turned their backs on him and even conspired to kill him. King David asked himself in ***Psalms 42:5***, (KJV) "Why art thou cast down, O my soul? And why art thou disquieted within me?" He then told himself, "Hope thou in God: for I shall yet praise him, who is the health of my countenance, and my God." We must talk to ourselves. We must stir ourselves to give praise and thanksgiving to God, who will replace our disappointments and sadness with healthy smiles. A healthy countenance is a cheerful countenance. ***Proverbs 15:13*** (KJV) says, "A merry heart maketh a cheerful countenance."

One of the definitions of *merry* is *joyous*. A joyous heart simply is a heart full of joy. Put your hope and trust in God instead of man. You will find that you will not decline joy. Time and time again, people will fail you. I have faith in God, not in people. We are not capable of being perfect for each other in thought, deed or action. **Pray** and ask God to help you not to depend on people. Ask God to free your heart of people so you can be whole within yourself. Being able to express joy is our responsibility. If we are not joyful, everything we touch will have a funk to it. People are not going to want to be around us. People may sympathize with us concerning our circumstances, but they still would not want to be around us if we are miserable all of the time. I hear this phrase a lot in my line of business, "Bad things happen to good people." I have news for you! Bad things happen to *everybody*, the good, the bad and the ugly. When bad things happen, we do not have to behave like we are under a rock. We should stand on the Rock. That Rock's name is Jesus.

It is a misconception to think that if your spouse isn't happy, you can't be

Our life source comes from above, not from our spouses. If you are married, recently separated and or divorced, you must come to terms that it does not matter what your spouse is doing or has done. We must realize that our circumstances do not define who we are and they most certainly should not determine how we should live. The responsibility is ours to live a joyful quality life. It is our job to protect our hearts. ***Proverbs 4:23*** (TNIV) says, "Above all else, guard your heart, for everything you do flows from it." It is our job not to allow our hearts to be allied with misery, sorrow, hurt, and discontentment.

When married to my ex, I found myself not happy if he was not happy. It is a misconception to think that your status of being one in marriage means you have to be miserable because your spouse is miserable. I have never read it in the scriptures that God expects us to be on one accord with foolishness. Let your light so shine and maybe he or she will see the light. But if not, it is not our burden to be miserable because they are. Over the years, I have learned that situations and people should not dictate whether I am joy. It is the very opposite. My joy should affect and infect people which will ultimately influence my situations in life.

I spent years being miserable in my former marriage because I would put unfair expectations on my ex-husband. I would think that if he would meet my expectations, I would then be happy. What a waste of time! Placing unrealistic expectations on your spouse results in disappointment that will only consume your heart. ***Proverbs 13:12*** (KJV) says, "Hope deferred makes the heart sick." Since then, I have learned that grown people are going to act in accordance to how they have been formed. I have concluded that you can pray, fast, talk, holler, do an Indian dance or do something as drastic as putting a gun up someone's backside and pulling the trigger -- they will still be the same. Other than your spouse being weary of your verbal tsunamis and religious theatrics, the only thing different about them would be the hole in your spouse's behind. Unless there is some sort of supernatural intervention like when the Lord slapped Saul (who became Apostle Paul) off of his horse, blinded him and then came down from heaven and told him where to go and what to do, people are going to act in accordance with whom they are.

One of my favorite quotes of Mia Angelo is, "The first time someone shows you who they are, believe them." Let acceptance free your heart and *live*! Strategically work around their behavior and enjoy *your* life! If they put forth some effort to change, one week or two weeks isn't enough time to officially rearrange your heart for this supposed miracle. A good six months of consistent change in behavior is needed before you can even start to believe there's a real change. My point is to enjoy every day that God gives you, with or without your spouse changing. Do the things that you enjoy. When you do, it may be without him or her. Enjoy yourself, of course, in an ethical way. We need to learn how to pray for people, let them be, and go on and live our own lives.

I've heard a phrase that has a ring of truth to it: "No one can make us do anything, we choose to do the things that we do." It is true, however, when in relationship with others, they may behave in ways that would cause us to do things that are not our first choices. It might not be our first choice to do things without our spouse but it might be the best thing for us. One day I was pulling up into a pharmacy to park and found that the parking spaces available were limited. There was a parking space next to a car parked on the line that divided the parking space. It forced me to park on the line. Right then, I got a revelation. Even though I wanted to park neatly between my lines, I was forced to park in a way I wouldn't ordinarily park. God helped me to see that people will do things to force our hands in the scheme of life. We may be forced to go outside of what we know is best. We may have to search for the next-best alternative.

I could have found another pharmacy with a better available parking space. I could have waited in that parking lot for others to come out to get a better parking space. However, pressed for time, I was keeping to my scheduled appointment. My priorities dictated that my appointment was important to keep. My standards of not wanting to take up too much time for things that are not all that important was a factor. I rationalized that no law would be broken by parking on the line. We cannot control what others do, but we can control our choices. We can control being happy about whatever decision we choose, even if it is not our first choice. In summary, when being forced to choose something that is not our first choice, the **4D** step is helpful:

Decipher through and select what is most important
Do not compromise your standards
Do not break any laws spiritually or naturally
Decide and then accept your decision

In relationship with our spouses, for the most part, we want them to like and do the same things that we like and do. We may be able to spark an interest in a partner concerning things we like, and it is also possible that we will not. Often we must resort to a second choice. Some spouses, however, do not default to the next-best thing. They try to control their mates' interests. It is delusional and a waste of time to think that we can control our spouses' preferences. I would like to make a strong suggestion: if this applies to you, don't feel miserable because your spouse does not do cartwheels over your interests. Great News! You do not have to drop your interests because you are married. As much as we want to share what we enjoy with our spouses, we may have to be mature and relinquish that idea. Enjoy to the max the interests that you do have as a couple. But also enjoy to the max the rest of you and your interests! I invite you to ponder this thought; you are married but also an individual with special hobbies, passions, dreams and goals that make *you* a unique individual. <u>**Pray** and ask God to help you see that your happiness is not the responsibility of your spouse</u>. It is totally up to you.

Try your best not to be like the Roses in the movie "War of the Roses." He had his interest and she had hers. However, because they could not enjoy their own interests without trying to control or manipulate each other, things got ugly. One thing escalated to another. It progressed from bad to worse when she was hosting a fancy dinner party with prominent guests. He came into the house intoxicated, went into the kitchen, stood on top of the stove, unzipped his pants and aimed at her catered meal. When she discovered what was drenching the food she had passionately prepared, she got so angry with him that she left her guests and got into her big-wheel truck with the idea of making his cherished sports car into junkyard scraps. He got into the sports car with the hopes that she would not carry out her plan with him inside. She caught up to him and rolled that big-wheeler over the top of his sports car, crushing it like a can with him inside. He was bent over the steering wheel by the caved-in roof of his car. She then shoved the crushed, mangled car, spouse and all, into a brick wall. Their relationship ended tragically, as do many relationships. The Roses demonstrated so many true-to-life misconceptions. They did not know how to let each other be. They got lost somewhere in their selfish desires. Like so many of us, as a couple they were miserable. They ultimately did not enjoy their lives to the end.

And so the misconceptions that we have, may be the cause of our joy not being fulfilled in the way Christ promised. To cut off the life source of our misconceptions, we may need to identify and put a stop to God's principles being violated. We may need to investigate other possibilities that will take us outside of the box that chains us to unhappiness. For the sake of our happiness, we may need to rearrange our priorities in dealing with people, places or things. God's plan for us is to experience joy in all that we do. We are an imperfect species living in an imperfect society that should allow a perfect God to guide us and mature us beyond living in error. ***Urban Joy*** is a good book to help eliminate misconceptions that consume much of our lives. It is a book that can help deliver us from living an erroneous life, and it will simultaneously fortify us with the core ingredients of living a joyful life.

~ Joy Is Always Positive ~

Joy is always positive. I have met people from all around the world and one thing stays consistent regardless of race or culture, the expression of joy is always positive. The Russian comedian, Yakov Smirnoff said, "Everybody laughs the same in every language because laughter is a universal connection." It does not matter who you are or what continent you live on, being joyful is being positive. God is universal and His joy is for the entire world. Working in sales, I have done business with foreigners who could barely speak English and when they would struggle to communicate with me, joy would manifest through their struggle. Together, we would laugh and smile as we came to some understanding. I have also worked with foreigners who struggled to communicate, and as they would speak, frustration, rude gestures, distrust and so on would be demonstrated. The atmosphere would be filled with negativity. This fact remains, if you house negativity, you will not be joyful. This stands true throughout the four corners of this world. Do not be deceived, we cannot suppress negativity and think that we are going to be joyful. Much like oil and vinegar, the two don't mix. Joy is positive through and through, no matter race, creed, culture or personality.

If you consider yourself to be a serious person, that is all well and good if you house joy. However, please do not think that you are a joyful serious person if you are the following:

- mean to people
- controlling
- impatient
- "it's my way or the highway" type person
- "it's all about me" type person
- always find yourself complaining about people and life's situations
- always having to correct, adjust or fix something because things are never just right
- one to hardly have anything positive to say
- one to allow the subject of bad things happening, to be the catalyst of your conversations most of the time.

If you find that your behavior is consistent in any of the above ways, it is time to change. Change only if you want to be a joyful person and if you want to reap the benefits of being a joyful person. You will see that your life will be the better for it in your marriage, friendships, work relationships and dealings with people overall.

As parents, conveying this message to our little adults can be challenging. Children can demonstrate being mean for many different reasons. We must recognize their little personal struggles and help them to identify what they are and then we can successfully navigate them to being positive. One year, my oldest daughter became intolerant of her little sister. She would treat her mean. Little sis wasn't having it so they would fight about everything. I literally mean about everything and everywhere, in the car, out of the car, in church, out of church, inside the house, outside the house, it did not matter. Sometimes their quarrelling sounded like two cats in heat. It bothered me tremendously. I wanted them to get along with all of my heart so I trained them to respect the scripture, "Be kindly affectionate one to another in brotherly love in honor preferring one another." ***Romans 12:10*** (KJV) Putting that scripture to heart, they could not justify being mean. They could not make excuses for fighting and they had to love each other, not just with words but with their actions of affection. They literally had to stop being selfish and consider each other. It took a little time to successfully get through this phase, but we did it.

My children respected scriptures because I started early in showing them that I respected the scriptures. I demonstrated that submitting to a higher authority is a good thing to do. If I messed up, I too would have to straighten up and do right. I also helped them to see that God is greater than any and every one on earth, including their parents. His love never fails and He is the authority for right living. If you are experiencing your children being mean, do not compromise. Hang in there, as parents we don't have to lose it when our kids act up. God's principles are an effective means to guiding your children to do right. The girls were mostly with me. As I stayed consistent and their father backed me, they would see that I meant what I said. Eventually they stopped fighting. They also would hug and kiss each other on their own.

They are both grown now. To this day, they both show love and affection towards each other. For example, Angela, once in her twenties, had a couple of wisdom teeth taken out. She waited too long to take her pain medication and was crying in agony. Stephenie, also in her twenties, was there caring for her sister, trying to make things as comfortable as possible. When realizing she could not stop her sister's pain, Stephenie started to cry too. Their love and affection for one another is proof that the word of God is a sure remedy. To this day, that scripture is branded on their hearts. I look forward to them teaching my grandchildren those life-changing words.

As parents or in any other position of authority, the expression of joy is always positive even when you have to bring down the hammer. Being in authority, you will always have to correct, adjust, and or train people. It is very possible to do this with a positive attitude. You can also speak on a matter for the purpose of getting better results with a positive attitude. Being mean and or moody is a whole different ball game. People will know the difference when you snap and bite them with your words. Being mean is being difficult. Being difficult is when you cannot let anything go smoothly. Being difficult, you will not take the humble approach of communicating properly. You will be short with people, curt, frank, rude, etc. Your being difficult may be caused by some personal struggle. Some examples of personal struggles are being hungry, impatient, tired, frustrated, sick, offended, in pain, insecure, jealous, controlling, hormonal, envious, vengeful, etc.

Handling matters through our personal struggles can cause people to leave our presence perplexed, hurt, crushed, belittled, frustrated, angry, argumentative, offended, bothered and so on. If you can remember times of difficulty you have experienced with people, I can pretty much guarantee that one or more of the personal struggles listed above is an underlying factor. I know too well about being in that place. I now pray and if I cannot release my personal struggle I get someone to quickly sober me. If you know you can be mean, **Pray** and ask God to help you to identify your personal struggles. Ask God to put the right people in your life to sober you. When we are being joy, we can never be mean. Being joy, we can express our concern about a matter, handle a matter and or deal with a matter and not leave people wrecked by negativity. We must recognize and get a firm grip on our personal struggles. I assure you that when we get a grip, we will find that our working and relating to people will be more productive. We have to stop justifying leaving people wrecked just because we believe that we are doing our job or we are directly telling people like it is.

I lost a dear acquaintance because of my personal struggle of being impatient. I left her wrecked. The truth was clouded by my personal struggle of being impatient. No matter how much I apologized, she did not bounce back. I valued our relationship more than the matter, but the damage was done. I have learned from that situation to tell myself to slow down when relating with people. Slowing down will help us to identify our own personal struggles and ultimately will help us to not take it out on people regardless of their shortcomings. We still talk from time to time, but the relationship is nothing like it once was.

Joy is always positive even if you are a direct person. You do not have to be mean. I know because I am a very direct person. As some say, "I shoot straight from the hip." I am one to nip things in the bud quickly so that progress and success is not hindered. I am a good perceiver. People cannot lie to me and it not be perceived before, after or during the lie. If something does not set right, I shoot straight to getting understanding. I do not like tucking issues away. I am a confronter. I do not like wasting life or time. I can be dominating, aggressive and assertive. Being this type person is not wrong, however, it can be wrong if I am always causing social casualties. . . such as people leaving my presence hurt, crushed, embarrassed, misunderstood, and so on. It takes temperance, patience, understanding, knowing the importance of proper timing, knowing when to let go and to let God, knowing how to choose my battles, sharpening my communication skills and not speaking everything that comes to mind. I had to be cultivated in a way that when I do speak, people are not leaving my presence messed up. In this level of maturity, I have come a long way and is still being perfected in it. I think it is going to be like that until I die and or when Jesus returns, whichever comes first.

I remember one time I had been so busy I did not do my online banking, and I did not check my bank account. Someone was making fraudulent withdrawals from my checking account. I did not catch it until six months later (Ouch!). Right after I discovered that problem and corrected it, my checkbook disappeared and was nowhere to be found. At the same time, the owner of our company had partnered with a particular bank that offered employees some nice benefits that I needed to research. Due to my busy schedule, I put a freeze on my accounts until I had time to investigate the missing checkbook and to see if the other bank's benefits were worth the effort of changing over. So that I would not be completely strapped for cash, my bank gave me access to my second checking account, which I was building up for a special event.

All of these things were happening around the time that my rent was due. The last day before the realty company would charge me a late fee was a Sunday. I called to report my dilemma. I wanted to know if I could bring them a check on that day, then on the following day bring them a check from the new bank if I decided to switch. The person who answered the phone was someone to whom I had never talked in the two years that I had been a resident. She was from the corporate office. She was very frank that there was nothing that she could do. She stated that I would be charged a late fee if I gave them a different form of payment the next day. She then stated that if I gave her a check today they had a machine that scans the checks and it would go straight to the bank immediately. I told her that I am not one to pay my rent late and is there a grace period for special circumstances like this. She stated that grace was given and a late fee will be charged automatically if payment is not made today. I told her that I did not believe that there was nothing that could be done. I asked, "What is closing time?" She said five p.m. I told her that I would be down there before closing.

When I went to the office, she immediately reiterated, "There was nothing that I could do." I replied, "I do not believe you." I also told her that confronting her was nothing personal and then explained that I ran a private school for fourteen years. I charged late fees. Late fees are set up to deter people from paying late. I know that under certain circumstances, late fees can be waived. She agreed and stated that she did not have the authority to make any decisions. I shared with her that I believed that she did not have the authority to waive or give graces, but I insisted that something can be done without penalizing me. I showed her three checks summing close to four grand that I had been waiting to deposit due to my accounts being frozen. I said, "Does this look like I cannot pay my rent of seven hundred and twenty dollars?" If she had any stereotypical racial profiling in her, it was annihilated. She then changed her entire demeanor and offered to talk to the corporate office tomorrow to see what they could do. At that point, I was done. I gave her most of my working cash on my cash card which left me strapped for cash until I got my banking straight. I made sure before I left that place she was laughing and smiling. She even later called me her new BFF (best friend forever). Even with me being direct, she did not leave my presence wrecked by negativity.

In order to live like this, through trial and error, I had to learn about people. People will try you because of their own personal struggles. We have to invest time in learning people so that they do not cause us to go sideways because of their own personal struggles. We cannot use the same methods, tones and gestures with everyone. We must distinguish the difference with the people that we can play with, and the people that we cannot (for various reasons). I have learned through trial and error that we should not handle matters frustrated. In all of the many facets of having to deal with people, the common denominator is to keep a positive attitude. By me being assertive and dominating, it is an ongoing process to humble myself quickly, especially being a woman. However, I stand firm on my standards of being treated with respect. Mean people do not like me. From time to time, I will have to rebuke them for disengaging their evil efforts towards me like Christ when He told Satan to "get thee behind me" while addressing Peter. ***(Mark 8:33)***

It is my daily practice to be positive, as well as, not cause people, especially men, to be “spun out” because of my strong, confident ways and methods. I had to learn that I can be myself around secure men. But with insecure men, I have to be creative, innovative and strategic. It is not my problem that they are insecure but it is my concern to handle them properly. We should take the time to make it a priority to know our strengths and weaknesses, as well as to know others' strengths and weaknesses so that we can handle them in a positive, joyful way. This should be a priority in our lives unless we are marooned on an unpopulated island. Then we only have to be joyful with ourselves.

Over the years, I acquired nick names like “Sunshine,” “Joy Bells,” and “Happy.” I obtained those names because I am mostly smiling, laughing and seeing the positive in a situation. It took some years of growth and maturity to get to this level. I stopped believing that I could not be joyful because of unfortunate situations or other people’s wrongdoing. This has made me so much more resilient. I started believing ***St. John 16:22*** (KJV) which says, “No man can take your joy from you.” It is my responsibility to remain positive and joyful. Just remember: everything we do, we choose to do it. We choose to get angry or express any other emotion that we care to express.

I am convinced that not being joy is my downfall; it will funk up my atmosphere, keep me in a negative mode and ultimately will make matters worse.

We do not honor the sacrifice of Christ when we choose not to be joy. He died so that our joy can be made full.

Being in Christ will help us to humble ourselves when we need to be humbled. Many times we are not joy because we will not humble ourselves concerning a situation. We do not want to let go of something that we should. Sometimes I have to be firm with myself and command myself to *let it go*! In Christ, we have an excellent maintenance plan to dwell peaceably with all men in joy. Some people do not want to let matters go, they are mean and bitter. If God did not make them your assignment to be used by Him to change them, leave them alone. Christ is the ultimate bookkeeper of life. If we follow his business plan concerning life, we can always stay in the positive.

When I gave my life to Christ, I erroneously, thought Jesus saved me from tribulation. Consequently with that mindset, every trial in my life caused me to feel like I was being attacked. I really did not have an understanding of ***Psalm 34:19*** (NIV) "A righteous man may have many troubles, but the Lord will deliver him from them all." When I would experience trouble, each time I would be caught off guard. I was not prepared. I would spiral down into negativity. I would be the more furious if the trouble was caused by someone that was close to me and or one of those so called "sanctified church folk." My attitude would be, "How dare they bring me this distress." I would be even the more heated to the point of wrath at times if I felt like they did it on purpose. Being immature, I thought if I acted positive about being handled poorly, people would walk all over me. I also thought that they would not know that they wronged me. I also believed that they would keep doing me wrong if I did not show them my other side. I was so wrong to think and behave that way. I discovered through much distress that my beliefs were far from the truth.

This next story testifies of my getting a breakthrough concerning my wrong thinking. I literally felt myself grow to another level of maturity right in the midst of being mishandled. Financially, this was a time when money was tough to come by. I asked my former pastor for a product that he was selling and I promised him that I would pay later. I sacrificially worked for him in the ministry and knew that he would understand me not having the cash right away. My income was little to none and I truly lived by faith. I called my former pastor's wife, as he instructed, to remind her to bring me the product when she came to church. I left a message on the voice mail. She got the message and instead of calling me, she called her secretary and instructed her to tell me that she got my message. She then said, "You better have the money if you want the product." When I got that message, I was "Smokin' Joe Frazier" angry. I felt like I was being treated like a stranger. She knew from past experiences with me that I was credible. I felt like her response was selfish and ungracious. I had done so much for the ministry and that stunt caused me to feel unappreciated. I felt like I was perceived as being a woman who did not keep her word. That whole message came across to me that I was trying to get over on her husband, the pastor, and she was the guarantor that I would not.

When we came out that evening to church, I made it obvious that I was put out with her. We got together and we hashed it out. Something that she said to me as we were talking, revolutionized my life. She initially took no claim to what was said, however, she then retracted and said, "If I did do it, **so what if I did?"** Those words played over and over in my mind, *So what if I did, so what if I did, so what if I did?* I think every smidgen of me feeling like a victim in the room that night was annihilated. It felt like I immediately grew some muscles of maturity. Instead of feeling like she was calling me out, that experience, reinforced in me a **So What?** No matter what people say or do, *So What*? I should still maintain my stability. I instantly felt that I no longer had a right to feel sorry for myself, act out, be mad, sad, or bad.

We can stay positive even when we do not like the actions of people. We can simply just do what we know is right. We should identify the characters of the people that we are dealing with and let it be no burden of ours as to how they choose to behave. Times will present themselves when people will say and do things that will make you want to take their heads off. Owning the revelation of ***Urban Joy***, you will notice that joy always presents itself as well. During times of these type temptations, look for your Joy AC Adapters and go to the sober people in your life that will help you to keep your head on straight. All confrontations and conflicts do not mean that you do not house joy. However, I suggest that you talk things over with the people that help you to think soberly before you confront anyone. The right people always help me when I am right at the brink of pulling out the ironing board to press people *out!*

One time, I was angry about an unjust deduction in my pay. The person responsible for this injustice came into my office to talk about something else. I was ready to spit nails with the intent of fastening him to a cross. Just before I did, my daughter Stephenie came walking into my office with a bouquet of flowers and a cute kitten card expressing her love and appreciation for me. It was no special occasion. It was just because. It melted my heart and that person was spared. I know that her coming was divinely orchestrated. God will intervene if we really want to live right. It is also a good thing to remember this comforting and convicting fact: Everyone pays for his or her actions. It is written that we will all pay for everything we do. ***(Revelations 20:12-13)*** We do not have to waste time and precious energy making sure people get what's coming to them.

It isn't a sin to feel angry about some of the horrible things that people do. ***Ephesians 4:26*** says, "Be angry, and do not sin": do not let the sun go down on your wrath." You can be angry and still be positive. You can express your disapproval and not become deviant. However, on a scale of one to ten, if you are angry more times than not, that means you are not handling life well. If you are always talking about your blood pressure going up because of your anger, you are not a positive person. People who are not positive are not joyful. They tend to be disturbed more times than not as if their panties are bunching and chafing them. Some tend to sit alone as if some ominous cloud is above them. Most of the time, no one really want to be around them. People tolerate negative people they don't enjoy them. Negative people latch hold to negativity like a parasite. If you can take it, ask the people who have to work with you and or live with you, "How often am I angry?"
Most Times ___
Sometimes ___
Rarely ___

If your answer is other than rarely, try not to justify, just change.

In maintaining our joy, it takes work to have a *So What?* attitude when people do wrong. It makes it easier to respond and not react. It should be a rarity that we are angry. Medical reports have proven that being angry often causes problems such as, ulcers, high blood pressure, migraines, heart conditions and other stress related ailments. If you find that you are always angry, **Pray** and ask the Holy Spirit to calm you.

Ask God to saturate your heart with the understanding that your anger will not bring about His righteousness. Ask God to help you see how to handle the matter. I have come to the realization that people really don't know what they are doing when they wrong me. ***(Luke 23:34)*** People who do wrong to others intentionally or unintentionally really don't fully know what they do. They are self-absorbed. It is a natural response to think that people are completely aware of their actions. However, think about when you were wronged by a person. Unless you share exactly how they have affected you, would they really know the damage they caused?

In order for us to effectively change regarding being positive, it is going to take faith. "Looking unto Jesus the author and finisher of our faith; who for the joy that was set before him endured the cross, despising the shame, and is set down at the right hand of the throne of God." ***Hebrews 12:2*** (KJV) Like Christ, our joy is set before us. Our faith in Christ will help us to endure our cross (troubles, trials, tribulations). No matter how much we want to act in a way other than joy, by faith we can endure. By faith we can live ***Urban Joy***. Joy is always present, and no matter how we feel, by faith, we can draw from it. The Apostle Paul said something so fitting to the Gentiles, "Now the God of hope fill you with all joy and peace in believing, that you may abound in hope, through the power of the Holy Ghost." Being filled with joy and peace from the God of hope, we will always be positive.

Joy is always Positive
"Always Positive" is life being joy

~ Importance of Practicing Joy ~

To excel at anything we do, we must practice. And we must practice to perfection. Michael Jordan practiced and finally the coaches stopped cutting him from the team. He proved to be one of the best basketball players in the world. It has been reported that movie stars with perfectly toned and shapely bodies, work out for eight hours a day with their personal trainers. They stay at it until they reach their goals. Any great musician passionately practices and his entire day is just about consumed with a love for music. Being a person with great joy is no different. You have to practice joy. It takes a faith-filled conscious effort to work at being joyful. ***James 2:22*** (NRSV) says, "You see that faith was active along with his works, and faith was brought to completion by the works." Verse ***24*** (KJV) says, "See then how that by works a man is justified, and not by faith only." In a nutshell, it is very ineffective to say, "I believe" and not do what we believe. Our beliefs must be practiced. The beautiful thing about practicing joy is that it is always fun and delightful.

Regardless of the number of times you tell yourself that you will maintain being joy and fail, remember this truth: "There is no failure in success." Let your determination activate something that I call a "Success Gene." I personally believe that everyone has a Success Gene." All it takes is the right resources, people, and methods to activate it. I see it clearly with people who have triumphed over many obstacles and are sharing their gifts, talents and skills with the world to name a few, Dr. Martin Luther King, Dr. Bill Hamon, Michelle and President Obama, Joel Osteen, Oprah Winfrey, Joyce Myers, Cher, Anthony Hopkins, TD Jakes, Colonel Sanders, Steve Harvey, Judge Mathis, and so many others, allowed their "Success Genes" to be activated and did not stop because of their failures and adversities. Steve Harvey and Tyler Perry both reported that they were once homeless. They both are now millionaires.

God has no respect of persons; He has given all of us the ability to succeed from any given level. If you fail, just get back up until you succeed. I cannot tell you the number of times I told myself that I would not get angry and act a fool. However, when the next opportunity arose for me to demonstrate joy during a trying situation, I did the very opposite. I headed straight to *Foolsville* and would act just like the *Foolians* would act. However, I did not let acting like a fool take me completely off course. Don't give up! Take things day by day, hour by hour, and minute by minute. My boss, AB, who was probably quoting someone, once said in a meeting, "It is a cinch by the inch and hard by the yard." That is such a true statement. The more you have faith to be joyful, the more you will work every inch of the way to be joyful. I did not get the reputation of being joyful because I have some special gift. I have it because I work at it daily on purpose. I may get angry about the evil deeds of others from time to time, but I am no longer quick to respond foolishly. I have adopted certain methods.

1. I slow myself down by praying and asking God to help me not to act out. I ask God to give me the right things to say if or when I have to address the matter.

2. I also slow myself down by talking over the unfavorable situation with someone that I know is stable and wise.

3. I take on the heart of God by forgiving and remaining merciful.

God says, "I will not cause my anger to fall on you. For I am merciful, says the LORD; I will not remain angry forever." ***Jeremiah 3:12*** (KJV)

Practicing being joy takes practicing spiritual principles that will take us out of our comfort zones. Your natural inclinations will not take you out of your comfort zone, especially during trying times. Your natural inclinations will not guide you to exercise for an hour, not to mention eight hours as some movie stars do. A former NBA player got into trouble because his inclinations told him he did not have to practice. Unlike that NBA player, we have to practice the word of God no matter the sacrifice, no matter how much it puts a strain on our ego, pride, feelings, etc. Being great can be likened to being great joy; they both take much effort, but the rewards are wonderful. Being joyful, people will want to be around you. A large percentage of people are always glad to see you. The other small percentage of people who aren't glad to see you aren't glad to see anyone.

I can personally tell you that it pays off to be joyful. You get so much favor from your boss, employees, merchants, customers, family, friends, etc. Over the years my employers have happily done for me above and beyond what was expected of them. As a matter of fact, I have experienced the same with my employees and merchants. As a woman, it feels like a great accomplishment to get discounts, sales and mark offs for quality items. I like shopping at Macy's for that very reason. My son-in-law jokes about Macy's stock going up when I shop there. It is common for me to get to laughing and conversing with the wonderful Macy's workers, and before I know it, they gladly serve me and find coupons so that I could get a greater discount. One special time, Angie's mother-in-law, Cindy, and Cindy's mother, Mimi, were here in Charlotte to visit. Angie was pregnant at the time. She was at the stage when she had to eat or she would feel sick. The kind Macy's worker who was laughing and talking with us realized my daughter's predicament and she went into her lunch pail and gave my daughter her trail mix bar. That was so kind of her. It saved the day, and we were able to stay and shop more. You find more favor when you are joyful.

When I go into the restaurants that I frequent, the people there are always happy to see me and happy to serve me. I have even had chefs tell me to ask for them because they want to make me something special not listed on the menu. Being in sales, people buy from me mainly because of how the joy emanating out of me make them feel. After the sale, they even go out of their way to bring me things, bake me goodies and buy me gifts. They even invite me to some of their social events. Being joyful reaps the same results with family and friends. My invitations are sincere. Family and friends entreat me to come rather than praying that I don't show. I always find they want to treat me or bless me. Joy is always positive, and I find that being joyful pays off in every area of my life.

However, being joyful comes with a warning label. Once you buy into being joyful, mean people will not like you; people who are not joyful on a constant basis will conclude that you are off your rocker. When you enjoy laughing so much that you laugh a little longer than everyone else you will be viewed as "cuckoo for Coco Puffs." When you choose to smile, sing and be happy instead of being moody, mean, grumpy, critical, judgmental and/or sad, some people will conclude, perhaps even comment, that you are disruptive. People huff and puff and ask you why you are smiling, singing or acting so happy . . . and they do it in a disgruntled tone. People accept loud fussing, often even finding it entertaining, but shouting something in joy is another matter. People will react as if it is obnoxious. God's word supports laughter, merriment and shouting with joy. It is so beneficial to our health, atmosphere and success. God's word discourages all negative emotions mentioned above because they set us back. Practicing joy, you must divorce yourself from people's comments and facial expressions. Being concerned about what "they" think has no payoff. Being joyful will activate your "Success Gene," and I cannot say this often enough: **It pays off.**

I remember one time, my daughter Angie and some friends had gotten tickets to see Christian Comedians who had come to Charlotte. My daughter invited me to come. I was elated because I wanted to go, but she was not sure if she could get me a ticket at such late notice. I said to her, “I accept your invitation, and I am going to get a ticket.” I said those words with confidence because I felt that God was going to make a way for me to attend the show. There had been all kinds of things that were not funny going on in my life, and at that time, I really could have used a concentrated dose of laughter.

When my daughter got to the theater, she went to the ticket counter to get my ticket but they told her that the show was *sold out!* I had already gotten dressed, left work and was headed towards Charlotte when she called to tell me the seemingly bad news. My faith would not let me turn around. I told her with even greater confidence that I was still coming and that I was going to get a ticket. When I finally arrived in the city, I went to the Blumenthal Theater. This man dressed nicely in a pressed suit came up to me as I approached the entrance of the theater. He asked me if I was coming to see the comedy show. I said, “Yes.” He shared with me that it was at the Knight Theater and then told me how to get there. He did not work there. It was a little strange. It seemed like a divine intervention because he walked right up to me and gave instructions. I was really tempted to think that he was an angel because shortly after speaking with him, I looked back and he was nowhere to be found.

When I found the Knight Theater, I had to park in a huge underground parking facility directly across from the theater. Once I came to the surface exiting the parking lot, I ended up on a street that had me completely turned around. I was not that familiar with the city. I was lost. I had to ask people on the street for directions. I had to do some walking in my high heels and it was hot. I did not mind so much because I looked really nice, I had on a really cute dress. I turned some heads in Charlotte that day. I felt like a supermodel using the streets of Charlotte as my runway. (I can dream, can't I?) Ok, I will eliminate the super in supermodel and simply say a really good-looking role model of a mom in her late forties. Is that better? Ok, back to the story.

Half an hour later I arrived at the theater. I was late, hot and my feet were saying "Lady, get off of me!" The usher asked me for my ticket and when I told him I did not have one he guided me to the ticket counter. With a smile, I told this man that was behind the counter who was not smiling, that I needed to buy a ticket. Still not smiling he said, "Sold out." I said, "Oh no, pleasantly, you do not know what I went through to get here." He just stared at me with his wide brown eyes and a blank expression. But the woman next to him said, "What do you mean?" I told her my story and she called one of the ushers over and told her to escort me to one of the reserved front seats. I went to pay her and she said, "No Charge!" I thanked her with joy and excitement! She smiled. My joy paid off, that reward was great! I got in for free . . . and got a really good seat. I sat in that seat with poise, very honored to be one of God's VIPs. It was a really good show, I got just what I needed. I laughed and laughed and laughed some more.

I had many personal struggles surrounding this event. I had to travel a distance knowing that the event was sold out. I went to the wrong theater blocks away, I got lost coming up from the parking lot, I had to walk a few blocks in the heat and in high heels, my feet began to hurt, I was late and alone. I could have easily been frustrated, discouraged and could have given up. I could have easily behaved with a bad attitude. God wanted to bless me, however, I had to stay in faith and practice working joy in order to receive my blessing. I am so very glad that I did. That evening was truly a blessing. Many of us miss out on our blessings because of our bad attitudes and many of us blame not actually receiving our blessings on people or on the devil. But as my mom used to say, "Ain't no devil, it's you!" Housing a bad attitude will hinder your blessings. Practicing joy causes your blessings to continuously flow.

Practicing joy comes with instructions. Remove yourself from a situation, if you find that you will not to be joy. **Pray** and ask God to give you the strength to walk away. **Pray** against offense entering your heart as well as any after thoughts that would cause you to want to go back and stir up the matter. Ask God to saturate your heart with ***Psalms 119:165*** (KJV) which says, "Great peace have they which love thy law:

and nothing shall offend them." Removing yourself takes discipline. Those of us who would love a beautiful body we must *remove ourselves* from the cakes, cookies, breads and rich foods. (*Can I get an Amen!)* There is an account in the *Bible* that tells a story about a man named Joseph. He *removed himself* from the King's wife who wanted him to lie with her. The King trusted Joseph. Joseph *removed himself* by running away. Joseph was a godly single man. I am assuming that he did not have a woman to fulfill his sexual needs, but he ran away from that opportunity because he knew that it was wrong to consent. If you feel that you no longer have the volition to express your joy and things are almost forcing you to consent to acting out, like Joseph, **remove yourself.** Run, "Run, Forrest," run to the way of escape that God has made for you to maintain being joy. ***1 Corinthians 10:13*** (KJV) says, "There hath no temptation taken you but such as is common to man: but God is faithful, who will not suffer you to be tempted above that ye are able; but will with the temptation also make a way to escape, that ye may be able to bear it."

When Joseph ran from that woman, some may think that Joseph suffered from *eurotophobia* (fear of female genitals). Some may think he was a punk. I think Joseph was wise. Exercising wisdom and removing yourself from a situation does not mean that you are a punk, wimp or noodle-back. It means that you are choosing to do the right thing and it will pay off like it did for Joseph. There are a few certainties in life.

Practicing joy of a certainty
will set you up for life.
It Pays Off.

~ *Ways to Practice Joy* ~

To practice joy, the *Bible* supplies us with fun things to do, especially when we find ourselves a quart low. One thing that we can do (which we really do not think to do) is to leap. Now wait! Before you think that my cheese fell off the cracker or my elevator didn't go all the way up to the top, leaping is a Biblical principal. ***Luke 6:23*** (KJV) states that we should "… leap for joy." I remember the first time that I actually took this scripture literally and tried leaping for joy when I needed to stir my joy. I tell you with all sincerity, it worked. Initially I felt silly because I did not feel a spark of enthusiasm which is normally what would cause me to want to leap. I ignored how I felt and started to leap. Before I knew it, I was laughing. I thought partly because I felt silly. I also knew that leaping is a Biblical principle that strategically caused my negative feelings to be overtaken by joy.

Leaping for joy is not so unusual. We see it all of the time but it is not something ordinarily talked about, it is just done. How many times have you seen someone leap when something good has happened? We leap when a loved one walks through the door; we leap at a ball game when players do something spectacular. For years we have been seeing people leap on games shows. Leaping is a natural response that can activate a spiritual principle. I have a suggestion for married couples: try leaping for joy right in the middle of an argument. Why not? You need joy to overcome some of those heated discussions. It may seem foolish but I promise, things will turn comical. ***1 Corinthians 1:27*** (KJV) says, "But God hath chosen the foolish things of the world to confound the wise ..." If your children are acting testy, have them leap or you leap. They are going to break and laugh. As a whole, we do not do much leaping unless there is some strong emotion of enthusiasm. If we want to practice joy, then we should leap more often.

When my daughter Stephenie was around twenty-three years of age, we went to the Cleveland County Fair in North Carolina. We were having fun kidding around. We were laughing at the little performing dogs and people walking around eating these gigantic, prehistoric-looking turkey legs. I was secretly being bad by mocking this testy little man, who was about ninety-eight pounds wet, with a miniature whale I had won at a game. I started mocking him because he was being mean to people while operating the shooting game. He was very snappy, telling people if they did not like the game they could leave. It would not have been appropriate for me to correct him, so I pretended that my whale was biting his butt as he was biting people with his words. Stephenie just laughed and took pictures as I was making fun. After having fun taking pictures of the little testy man and my whale, we continued to walk through the fair.

A band played in the center of a large, spacious building without four walls. Inside, there were bleachers with no one present Maybe they were setting up for a future event. Spontaneously I got the thought of Stephenie being a dancer for years, so I dared her to go in and dance before the band like she was invited. She accepted the challenge. As I recorded, she took off leaping in there like a gazelle. It looked so funny. She and I laughed until our bodies were limp like we were puppets on strings. She could barely dance because she was so tickled. Leaping for joy is a carefree light way of having fun and practicing joy. I still have that moment on video and from time to time I would watch it for a good laugh. Leaping looks funny and it feels funny. Leaping for joy is a Biblical truth that seems odd when we are not enthused but it is effective in causing joy to erupt.

Another fun way of practicing joy is to shout. ***Psalms 35:27*** tells us to *shout for joy.* To some, shouting is so impolite. To God, shouting is one of the things that we can practice to maintain our joy. I enjoy shouting because it is fun and it also helps to release ungodly stress and pressure. I remember when I was an adolescent I would shout sometimes just because I felt like it. It must have been a hormonal rush. My girlfriend and I would laugh about it every time. If I still have not convinced you, try it. Shout a happy thought and observe how you feel. Shout something fun. Shout, "I love you, Lord!" If you are bold enough to do it, examine how you feel. Did you experience a welling up inside of you? Did you automatically smile when you did it? Don't think that shouting is silly or insignificant, because the walls of Jericho came down with a shout mentioned in ***Hebrews 11:30.*** Have you ever noticed at a ball game, the people seem happy during the game. They are shouting and loving it. They are dancing and smiling when the camera spotlights them. Now after the game, please only pay attention to the fans of the winning team if you still want to see joy. Maybe if we shout congratulations to the fans of the winning team as they pass by, it would stir up our joy. Yeah, right! How often will we see that?

Shouting is a Biblical principle that is an outburst of emotion to practice joy.

Psalm 32:11(KJV) says, "Be glad in the Lord and rejoice, you righteous ones, and shout for joy all you who are upright in heart." The part of the verse that says, "be glad in the Lord and rejoice" is a directive. It is not worded in a way where it is asking us to be glad and rejoice; it is telling us to do it. This scripture also reveals that to practice joy by shouting, our hearts must be upright. Shouting when arguing or when you are angry is fruitless. You will not get anything but a headache and or a bad experience.

One time when I was fairly new at driving, I was lost, nervous and could not think while trying to understand the poor directions that were given to me. I was going about 15 mph below the speed limit, trying to look at the directions while squinting to see addresses and street names. Traffic was backing up behind me. A car on the opposite side of the road slowed down, a man rolled his window down got my attention and shouted *a** hole*! I do not have to spell it out, do I? I was already as nervous as a cat on a hot tin roof. When he shouted those words, the impact was like a punch in the face and I immediately cried. It really got to me because I rolled my window down thinking he was stopping to help me. I am sure he felt like he was doing a good deed by representing the people behind me. His heart was not upright when he shouted those words and joy was not felt.

If you find yourself shouting and it is not for joy or with an upright heart, put on the brakes. It happens. Stop speaking. Maybe count to ten in your mind, inhale, do something that will help you to simmer down. My former sales manager, Jeff, aka "Boom-Shaka," had a tendency to lose his cool. To keep himself in control, he would sometimes stop speaking right in the middle of a sentence, close his eyes, stretch out his hands like he is about to meditate and he says a little above a whisper, "Woosaaaaaah!" His tone and attitude would change immediately for the better. I admired his efforts and at the same time, I laughed every time because I know too well what he was experiencing.

When our hearts are upright, positive, and filled with the right things, shouting is delightful. We will be light-hearted and will have fun. I can't help but feel joyous when people shout an affirming phrase when I do things such as sing, wear something nice and or get a strike. When phrases such as "Woooo!" and or "Get it Girl!" are shouted, it makes me happy. I can't help but to cheer inwardly when my managers lift their voices and call me a "Beast" with some bass in their voice. I feel like I am really doing a good job. Save your shouting for joyful moments. Save your shouting for encouragement, not discouragement. God intended for shouting to benefit us not tear us down.

Shouting is not exclusively a "churchie" thing, as some church folk would think, it is a universal thing. I must admit, it is wonderful when the Spirit of God falls in a service and I am compelled to shout "Thank You Lord," "I love you Lord," or "Glory Hallelujah." I believe praising God is what I have been created to do inside and outside of the church. However, for some people, shouting is a dance done in the church with organ music playing to stir the soul. You do not need organ music or break out in a shoe scuffing dance to shout. As long as your heart is upright, you can be free to practice joy by shouting anywhere as long as it is in decency and in order.

I have seen people shout things that would give them some sort of pleasure but it would not be decent nor in order. For example, I have heard people shout *whale!* when they saw an overweight person or they would shout *bomb!* in a public place and think that it was so funny. Someone told me that when he was younger a few of his friends would ride by AA meetings after drinking. As the members came out, they threw beer bottles at them, shouting words to encourage them to go back to drinking. Of course they thought it was hilarious to see the looks on the struggling AA members' faces. Shouting things when your heart isn't upright will have an adverse effect on people. Shouting for joy causes light heartedness, delight and everyone is blessed.

Singing is another wonderful way of being joyful. ***Isaiah 65:14*** (KJV) says, "Behold my servants shall sing for joy." Singing stirs the soul. It is a method that God created to bring comfort to His creation. The right song can turn a dull moment into a burst of refreshing vitality. Singing for joy will bring on a sense of happiness. Singing will bring more meaning to life and life's situations. Singing worship songs helps to usher in the presence of the Lord and in the presence of the Lord is the fullness of joy. ***(Psalm 16:11***) I can't count the times, I have kicked bad feelings in the face by opening up my mouth and singing songs to the Lord. I would feel an overwhelming warmth, comfort and feeling of love. I would just sing on my job or other places and the temptation to feel bad would diminish. I would be filled with His glory. One of the definitions of *glory* is the *bliss (*spiritual joy*) of heaven.*

Every time my grown, muscular, manly-man brother, Tim, would wake me with singing his elementary song, "Good morning to you, good morning to you, we're all in our places with bright shiny faces..." it would be refreshing and I could not help but laugh because it didn't fit his appearance. His singing helped me to wake up on the right side of the bed. In the morning, singing unto the Lord is a wonderful way of starting our day no matter what side of the bed we wake up on. At the Christian Academy, we purposely scheduled chapel early because it set the mood for the students and staff. We would sing and rejoice and when it was time to go to class, everyone who participated was happy and ready for the day. But the students who resisted during chapel always found their day challenged by some negative emotion. Singing in the morning helps. As a mother, I loved raising my girls in that type of environment. I thank Dr. James for being obedient to his divine purpose by opening the school. I thank God for the opportunity to fulfill my divine purpose by running the school. Singing was definitely a major source of why our school was a happy school. All of my school babies are mostly grown now. They are out on their own and many are doing well.

There are many things that I miss about my baby Stephenie living with me, but the one thing I miss the most is hearing her sing. Throughout the day, she would sing. It did not matter where she might be, she would sing. All over the house, in the car, on vacations, in the yard. . . it didn't matter, she would sing. Everyone's mood would be pleasant when she sang. She would not do it for an audience or attention. It naturally just flowed out of her. Her melodies would echo from room to room. She would sing whatever came to mind. Some of it would be funny. Her songs could be about anything to which she might put a melody -- like toilet paper or putting on her pantyhose. I would not let her hear me laugh at times because I did not want her to stop. It was a joy to hear her sing. Many times she would break out singing praise and worship songs. She was so inspirational that there were times that our entire family would join in throughout the house and we all would sing. Those precious memories I will always cherish.

Parents, if you want your children to have a better temperament, sing together as a family. It does not matter if none of you can carry a tune. When my daughters were young and had to sit in the back seat of our vehicle, I would sing songs to keep their mood up. I remember I made up a song called, *Do You Have Any Black-Eyed Peas*. It was upbeat. They would clap and it went something like this:

> Do you have any black-eyed peas
> Do you have any black-eyed peeee-eas
> Do you have any black-eyed peas
> Do you have any bla-black, black-eyed peas.

Ok, I don't expect any accolades for those lyrics, but we would sing it over and over . . . sometimes all the way to our destination. We enjoyed singing that silly, simple song. But the joy that sprang up in our hearts wasn't silly, and the bond that we shared wasn't simple at all. We shared a depth that is even felt today.

I love this scripture: "Praise ye the Lord, sing unto the Lord a new song, and his praise in the congregation of the saints. ... Let the saints be joyful in glory. Let them sing aloud upon their beds." ***(Psalms 150:1-5)*** When we sing, we release melodies from our heart. When we sing a new song, we release a newness of heart. It is as if we wash away the old, stale things that lie stagnant in our hearts and we get refreshed. "Sing psalms, hymns, and spiritual songs, singing with grace in your hearts to the Lord." ***(Colossians 3:16)*** Everything that we do, we should do it unto the Lord. When we sing, be it spiritual songs, a new song, and songs celebrating life and life's situations . . . or even silly ditties about black-eyed peas, we are practicing joy.

Psalms 126:2-3 (KJV) says, "Then was our mouth filled with laughter, and our tongue with singing... The Lord has done great things for us; whereof we are glad." Singing is one way and laughter is another wonderful way of practicing joy. When we are in touch with the fact that God is greater than what we are going through, God has done great things for us, then we can be glad and our mouths can be filled with laughter. Laughter brightens our countenance and our hearts. Laughter is the best medicine in the world. Norman Cousins, a writer known for his humor, said, "Hearty laughter is a good way to jog internally without having to go outdoors." We should laugh even when we do not feel like it and watch the power of joy take effect. Laughter is a catalyst that will springboard us right into a joyous attitude. "I believe that laughter is a language of God and that we can all live happily ever laughter" -- Yakov Smirnoff.

Laugh when "snuffen" is funny. The word "snuffen" came about when I was in my early teens. My girlfriend and I were in church sitting next to my mom and her Spanish husband. We had the giggles, as usual, this time because of a grandmother and her very young granddaughter. They were sitting in front of us, and they made church a comedy hour that day. The little girl had a very dark complexion with full light-pink lips. (She favored the Looney Tunes character Marvin the Martian, who always talked about his space modulator.) Her lips and that small white piece of paper had a thing going on. Together, they were doing all kinds of silly things that struck us as comical. The grandmother's expression showed she had enough of that nonsense. Her neck stiffened, and her eyes shifted in a way that a mother's eyes get when they are about to inflict pain with where the good Lord split us.

Unbeknownst to the little girl, occupied by her own silliness, the grandmother would lift her fist high above the church pews, aiming for the girl. We couldn't see where her fist landed, but we knew it made contact because her granddaughter's body jerked. Surprisingly the little girl did not cry. She screeched a high pitched animal-like sound, like a squeaky toy, as the white piece of paper plunged from her lips. The worst thing for us was that they repeated this three times, and each time it was as funny as the first time. It was like the movie "Ground Hog Day." We laughed and laughed and laughed and then laughed some more. My mom's husband was sitting next to me. He looked down at me with his wrinkled, thick, bushy eyebrows and said with much expression, "Top it, top it. *Snuffen's* funny!" When he said that with his strong accent, like silly young girls, we laughed so hard that tears rolled down our cheeks and our bodies looked like we were having fits while no sound escaped our mouths. It was one of those hard, silent uncontrollable laughs. It seemed impossible for us to stop.

First of all, we knew that we should not have been laughing in church. One of the worst temptations for me is to keep from inappropriate laughter when something strikes me as funny. Secondly, he kept looking at us with such a look of repulse, but we were too far gone to care. Thirdly, he botched up the words "stop" and "nothing" so badly that it could have been a skit off of *Mad TV*. Our laughing was terrible, and the timing could not have been worse, for it was during one of those quiet times in church. No one was singing or clapping; nothing that made noise was going on. We could not blend our laughter and behavior with other sounds. The people were *Shhhh-silent*. The laughing was so bad that my mom leaned over with her lips drawn back, her teeth gritting, and said, “Get Out!” For the remainder of the service we had to sit in the foyer. So I literally was kicked out of church for laughing. That is an example of a good thing turning bad.

Since then, I have used the phrase “snuffen’s funny” whenever people act a little too tight. Laughter is such a fun way to practice joy. Laughter refreshes us with a hormone called endorphin. This hormone has a tranquillizing effect and relieves pain. Laughter causes naturally healthy things to happen. Endorphin is secreted by the brain. Laughter is like jogging internally. It strengthens the immune system. It gives us energy. It stimulates the heart and blood circulation. Laughter is one of God's ways of keeping us healthy. ***Proverbs 17:22*** (KJV) says, “A merry heart does good like a medicine.” *Merry* means *full of cheer or gaiety, joyous, pleasant, jolly, jovial. Jovial* means *endowed with or characterized by a hearty joyous humor; a spirit of good fellowship. Humor* means *the ability to perceive, enjoy, or express what is comical or funny*.

Have you ever seen someone trying to resist laughter when something is really funny? I am not talking about something distasteful. I am talking about something clean and funny. Resisting laughter hinders joy. Laugh even when you do not feel like it. It is a benefit It keeps you healthy, light-hearted, pleasant and joyful. If you are one to struggle with being able to enjoy what is comical or funny, you must have faith that you can laugh even if you do not feel like it. Having faith will position your mind to believe in the ability to perceive, enjoy, or express what is comical or funny. If it is not a matter of life and death or someone getting hurt, just let it rip . . . laugh. Look for the humor in anything.

Another fun day at the Christian Academy, one of my teachers came to me appalled and told me that some of the daycare four-year-olds and the K-5 students were calling each other *holes*. I said, “Holes? What do they mean by saying holes?" She then proceeded to tell me that she did not want to repeat what they said. I asked, “Was it that bad?” She said, “Yes, it is vulgar.” I then said, “Well in an around-about way, tell me what I need to address.” She proceeded to tell me that they were calling each other “A” hole and "B" hole, pie holes and hinny holes. I tried my best to keep a straight face while she was telling me this with disgust because after all, these are little Christian four- and five-year-olds. We called for an assembly. During the assembly I tried my best to reprimand them. I told them that what they were saying was vulgar and that they were using curse words.

But as I looked at their innocent faces, I could not imagine those words coming out of those little mouths. As I would try to tell them that we should not call each other names, I would lose my voice trying to hold back my laughter. I would make assorted throat noises trying to keep from laughing. The students got wise to what I was doing and began to chuckle. I believe God got me through that assembly. How can you hold an assembly reprimanding the entire student body and releasing laughter at the same time? Housing joy is the answer. We must practice laughing; it is one of the ways that will keep us joyful, especially during the times when we have to bring down the hammer.

This next story falls under the category of laughing when *snuffen's funny:* My daughter Angie picked me up from work one night. As usual, I greeted her cheerfully. She looked at me and immediately burst out with tears and muttered words. My heart sank. I said, "Ang, Ang, what's the matter?" I started asking one question after another. She shook her head back and forth, gesturing "no" and muttering words really fast. I said "Ang, please slow down. Tell me what's wrong." She finally calmed down enough to articulate, "I just hit a cat and I think that I killed it." I said with relief and sympathy at the same time, "Oh, no, I am so sorry." We had recently gotten her a kitten so I knew this was devastating to her. So I asked, "Are you sure you killed it?" While crying, she stated, "Yes." She described how she felt her wheels roll over it. I began to tear up as she told me. She began to drive to exit the parking lot.

The parking lot was illuminated with bright stadium lights. As we looked in a distance, we saw this big red object, strangely smack-dab in the middle of the parking lot. We had no idea what it was. It was odd and appeared out of place, whatever it might be. As we got closer we intensely inclined our faces towards the windshield with curiosity. It became clear as we rode by. It was a very nice-sized butt and legs of a woman wrapped in tight red Capri pants hiked in the air. The size of her butt covered her head, face, and arms. She was bending over doing something. It looked like one of those garden ornaments but only red and real. With both of our faces wet with tears, we immediately broke out with intense laughter without one word spoken. Out of curiosity, we leaned our faces all up in that woman's goodies, not realizing until we got up close that it was her behind. *That* was funny.

We laughed for a few minutes; Angie felt so much better. I then said, "God knows just what we need during horrible situations." We went back to the scene of the accident. Unfortunately the kitty was a goner. Angie could not bring herself to move it, so I got out and put it in a resting place. I got back in the car; because of the laughter, she was no longer crying and could stomach the harsh reality of the accident. I believe if she would have resisted laughing, she would not have gone through that tragedy as well as she did. I cannot stress enough that laughter helps to get us through the harsh realities of life. There was *snuffen funny* about her accidently killing the kitty, but God has a way to set things up in our life so we can laugh during those horrible tragic times in our life.

God has given us some really great ways in His word to practice joy. We can leap, shout, sing and laugh.

Practicing joy will keep our joy buff like weight lifters who bench press every day. We will be strong and resilient.

~Joy is Connected to Our Obedience ~

It would make anyone curious enough to ask, "Why is my joy connected to me obeying someone or something?" It is common to think, "It makes more since that if I do what I want when I want, I would be happier." Obedience is a spiritual principle that keeps us in line, civil, considerate, humble and believe it or not, joyful. As a result of our obedience, some really cool things happen that cause our joy to flow. ***John 15:10-11*** (KJV) Jesus says, "If ye keep my commandments, ye shall abide in my love; even as I have kept my Father's commandments, and abide in His love. These things have I spoken unto you, that my joy might remain in you, and that your joy might be full."

According to ***John 15:10-11***, obeying God has wonderful benefits and rewards. One reward is that we abide in His love. The other is that joy will remain in us maximized to the fullest. Every human being is created to want and need love. Being loved will always bring pleasure and fulfillment. Knowing that an almighty, all-powerful, all-knowing God loves me is delightful. To some, obeying is an unpopular deed. To others, obeying is seemingly impossible. Regardless, it is a contingent fact that our joy is connected to our obedience. It would behoove us to make sure we have a full tank of joy to take us through life's long journey, instead of conking out midway when faced with adversity. God knows that we are creatures of habit. He created us. He knows that if we conform ourselves to reverence and obey Him, our pattern of behavior would trickle down into how we treat one another.

To obey Godly principles requires humility, and in doing so, we will experience peace, love, order and great achievement. While raising our daughters, we instilled in them the true-to-life fact that no matter how grown we get, someone is always going to tell us what to do. We will always have to obey someone or something. We also reinforced the principle that obedience reaps rewards while disobedience reaps consequences. We helped the girls to recognize that they were happiest when they obeyed. I did my best to exemplify that growing and succeeding in life will transition a lot smoother when rules are respected and obeyed. I am fully persuaded that God's intent is that we develop a true heart to obey Him, and then through him, we can obey those in authority in our home, work place and in society.

I Corinthians 14:33 (KJV) says, "God is never the author of confusion, but of peace..." If you find that things are a little chaotic or disruptive in your life, identify the spiritual principles you might be neglecting. Identify where you have excluded God. Correct the neglect, and obey. Just think about how *crazy* things get when children are disruptive to their parents, when husbands and wives are disruptive to each other, when employees become disruptive to employers, when athletes act disruptively to their coaches, and people are disruptive to the laws of the land. Being disruptive may be the cause of not liking someone or something. ***I Corinthian 14:40*** (KJV) instructs us to, "Let all things be done decently and in order." When this scripture is obeyed, things will become orderly as well as peaceful, and the flow of joy will not be hindered.

I run late a good portion of my life. It takes much effort for me to be on time and it takes good people around me to help me to be keen concerning time management. I remember when I had a haughty attitude about getting to work on time. I justified being late because management did not get there on time. My attitude was justified by the thought, "So why should I?" I would think, "If someone confronts me I am going to say something." I also declined being joy because I was consumed with negative thoughts of how to deal with management. God was not leading me to do that. God was leading me to humble myself and to give an account of why I was not on time. From that experience, am I now a punctual person? Does a chicken have lips? However, the experience eliminated my haughty attitude and I focused more on respecting the rules. Sparky Anderson (a Major League Baseball Hall of Fame manager) said, "The only thing I believe is this: a player does not have to like a manager and he does not have to respect a manager. All he has to do is obey the rules."

It is God's will that we be reverent to the rules of those in authority. ***Titus 3:1*** says, "Put them in mind to be subject to principalities and powers, to obey magistrates, to be ready to every good work…" (KJV) Most people in authority have done much to be in their position and the order that they are upholding is due respect. ***Romans 13:1-7*** (NIV) says, "Every person is to be in subjection to the governing authorities. For there is no authority except from God, and those which exist are established by God. Therefore whoever resists authority has opposed the ordinance of God; and they who have opposed will receive condemnation upon themselves. For rulers are not a cause of fear for good behavior, but for evil. Do you want to have no fear of authority? Do what is good. But if you do what is evil, be afraid; for it does not bear the sword for nothing; for it is a minister of God, an avenger who brings wrath on the one who practices evil. Therefore it is necessary to be in subjection, not only because of wrath, but also for conscience sake. For because of this you also pay taxes, for rulers are servants of God, devoting themselves to this very thing. Render to all what is due them: tax to whom tax is due; custom to whom custom is due; fear to whom fear; honor to whom honor."

Every position of authority is covered in these verses of scripture. It is plainly noted that God wants us to obey authority unto good works. We will be the better for it. For example, I got my first speeding ticket at the age of forty-nine. I can testify that I would have been a whole lot happier and richer, if I would have obeyed the speed limit. I was petrified in that court room. Every last one of us who received a citation looked busted and could not express one complaint as the judge and court officer sternly and frankly spoke to us about our offenses in front of everyone there. The judge and the court officer had the authority and the firearms to talk to us that way and the power to back it up. When I was called up to the judge, my hands and arm pits were moist from perspiring. I was so nervous. I am glad I had on a sweater to hide my body's reaction of being nervous. I do not ever, never ever never, want to go back to court again. My car runs so smoothly that I don't realize that I am well above the speed limit, so I now use cruise control. Speeding is a serious offense in the U.S. The speed limits are set up for our safety and protection. Some would still be alive today had they obeyed the speed limit.

On the other hand, God instructing us to obey does not mean that He isn't aware of people who abuse their authority. God is not saying that we have to be run over, controlled, and/or abused by mis-management, control freaks and or prejudice. From time to time, we will experience people who take their authority too far. Dr. Martin Luther King exemplified perfectly how to deal with the injustices of authority influenced by prejudice. To avoid being run over by cocky power seekers, we can appeal, relocate and or stand in faith that justice will prevail. For instance, my customer Roger lives in Clover, South

Carolina. He said, "The police there can be buttholes." I asked him, "Why?" He said, "They pull you over for nothin', even little old ladies aren't spared." He told me that one time he and his friend was driving 37mph in a 35mph zone. The police pulled him over and wrote him a ticket. The ticket literally was 2 mph over the speed limit. They went to court and the judge looked at the citation and said, "Really?" and threw the case out of court. My manager at the time, Lutz, chimed in on our conversation and said when he goes hunting in Clover, he makes sure his stuff is straight because those same police stop him for just looking out of the window. Even when authorities exercise character like harassment, racial profiling, being mean, offensive, etc., we can still obey what's right and not succumb to their profane behavior. No need to fear. We have laws and God to protect us. Our part is to make sure we do what's right. God has a way to turn things around in our favor when we depend on Him to bring us to justice.

Doing what's right is also obeying one another. God will use people to give words of wisdom so that things will be so much better for our lives. ***Ephesians 5:21*** (KJV) says, "Submitting yourselves one to another in the fear of God." We must live a life of humility. We would be so much happier if we would listen. Living almost a half of a century, I have seen young people and old who would refuse to listen to wisdom. The results would be horrible. I personally know of people who would not listen and because of it, they have been imprisoned or became homeless and now have very little quality of life due to poor choices. I have seen young adults blatantly disregard good counsel and to this day their lives are in shambles. I have seen coworkers come and go because time after time they would feel like they did not need to listen to the wisdom of their fellow workers. Their cockiness caused them to lose their jobs and the benefit of being employed. When we submit ourselves to one another in the fear of God, we stay in a place of accountability humility and even safety.

I remember a time when I worked with a Spanish young woman who dressed extremely sexily. She caught the eye of a Caucasian married man about twenty years older than she. They began to have an affair. The Lord impressed upon me to speak to this young women. The Lord told me to warn her that something really bad could happen if she did not stop messing around with the married man. He also impressed upon me to tell her to give her life back to Him and make things right with her children's father. I was very reluctant to approach her because I was not that close to her and the message was her personal business. But the Lord weighed on me so heavy because it was His business. God would not leave me alone. I went to her privately, personally shaken in tears. When I told her what God said, she cried and told me that she would stop and get it right. Unfortunately, she did not stop. The married man immediately upped his game by getting her an apartment and a car. She continued the affair.

About two weeks later, her children's father came up to our workplace. He waited for her to come out to the parking lot. He forced her and another co-worker at gunpoint into his car. They drove around for a while with him being enraged. He eventually let the co-worker out of the vehicle in center city. The co-worker immediately called the girl's family and police. The police did not find them until the next morning in an industrial area. Tragically, he blew her brains out and then turned the gun on himself. Those beautiful children are growing up without a mother and father and must live with knowing why they are without their parents. Side note: the married man did not shed one tear at her funeral as he sat, caressing and rubbing his wife and kids. I am glad that I obeyed but I am sorry that she did not.

Obeying one another is submitting to the authority of truth and wisdom. I love my boss, AB. One thing that I love about him is that he will take heed to the wisdom that I share concerning certain things. Even though he's the boss, he would humble himself, listen and agree. It doesn't matter what level of authority we have, we should never be too big to obey what is right regardless of the person saying it. There have been times that my daughters have given it to me straight, and as their mother, I would have to humble myself and listen because they were right. I am happiest when I listen.

Many husbands struggle with ***Ephesians 5:21.*** They believe that their wives are there only to submit to them. However, that belief is far from the truth. Whoever holds the authority of truth and wisdom is to whom we should submit. If a wife is in that position, a husband ought to listen. Victor Hugo, a French poet, stated profoundly, "It is often necessary to know how to obey a woman in order sometimes to have the right to command her." It is very difficult for a wife to obey a haughty, stubborn husband. I lived many years with a husband who was very stern about my obedience to him. But he lived a life of, "Do what I say and not as I do." If you are like that, husbands, it is not very effective to say the least. We will experience more harmony in our homes and with our spouses if we learn that we must submit to one another.

Ephesians 5:22, 24 (KJV) states, "Wives, submit yourselves unto your own husbands, as unto the Lord. Therefore as the church is subject unto Christ, so let the wives be to their own husbands in everything." This scripture is a "doozie" in a "Woman's World." I can hear some women cursing now if someone tries to tell them to obey their husbands. To some, obeying this scripture is like making a cat do standup comedy. Talking to, interviewing and counseling many women, I have discovered that as a whole we think that men are special, and not in an exceptional sense. We think that they all ride on a short bus. Men think differently than we do. We think that they are clueless to things that they shouldn't be clueless about. God is an all-wise God. He knows what it takes to humble us women. God knows that it is humbling to submit to someone riding on a short bus. Humility breeds harmony and harmony breeds joy/pleasure. God doesn't just throw words at us instructing us to obey. He gives us specific instructions on how to obey.

He instructs us to submit to our own husbands in everything. It is clear we do not have to submit to every Tom, Dick and Harry. It is clear that men will not have a community of women submitting to them. It is humbling for a man to only get it from one. God then tells us to submit in everything. This is where the cursing starts. But hold on! I know it is humbling, but this is where our thinking has to change. The first part of God's instructions tell us to obey our husbands as unto the Lord. When we see our actions through the eyes of pleasing God, it will be a whole lot easier to see the wisdom in obeying. The second part of that scripture gives an example of how the church is subject to Christ, so let us be to our husbands. Overall, the church respects and appreciates Christ for all that He has done for us. We should do the same with our husbands. We must show them that we appreciate all that they do.

There are many wives that are not happy and are not living a life of joy because they simply are not obeying their husbands unto good works. I am not talking about husbands who are taking their wives down paths of destruction or are mean, cruel, disrespectful, unreasonable, illegal, abusive, immoral, etc. God is not telling us to obey insanity and abuse. I am referring to husbands who are giving sound helpful advice or instructions like Christ, but their wives are not obeying and neither are they happy. Men are not as emotional as women; they can make sound decisions without emotion. For the most part, we as women go by what we feel, which is not always sound. We can be flighty and at the same time think we know it all. It is very humbling to have to submit. God knows that about us and wants us to remain humble. The truth is that some husbands leave their wives very frustrated for trivial reasons; they might ask their wives to help with things in the home or with the children; they might ask their wives not to let themselves go; they may ask their wives to clean the house, especially if they are home all day. They might ask them not to trash up the car; they might request the wives not have houseguests all the time; they might request intimate loving when they want it, and they might point out things that they feel put their wives or themselves in danger. These things are not unreasonable and can be remedied by simple obedience. However, many wives do not see these things as important and continue to disobey. This can cause turmoil and unhappiness in the marriage. A husband's responsibility is to secure, protect and keep order in his home. God has set forth this order. ***Ephesians 5:23*** (KJV) says, "For the husband is the head of the wife, even as Christ is the head of the church: and he is the savior of the body." Being obedient produces less drama and a whole lot more happiness for both husband and wife.

No matter what area of my life, during times I have been disobedient I have not felt God's approval or his complete hand of blessing. To the contrary, I felt as though things would never go right. I did not feel covered. As a result of disobedience, all my feelings are never good. Feeling bad causes me to decline my privilege of joy. I am concerned, not carefree. When I do what I know is right, I am happy and can sense God's approval. I know I can rightfully claim that all things will work out for my good. I am clear to see the favor of God over my life and am not clouded with the fear of the consequences of disobedience. I am sure I am protected. When I am obedient to what is right, I am humble, but when I am disobedient I am haughty, self-centered, and I justify my actions, all the while unhappy.

I have seen husbands behave the same way when expected to obey ***Ephesians 5:25-33.*** As I get older, I have seen from decade to decade, men struggling with obeying this scripture: “Husbands, love your wives, even as Christ also loved the church, and gave himself for it; That he might sanctify and cleanse it with the washing of water by the word, That he might present it to himself a glorious church, not having spot, or wrinkle, or any such thing; but that it should be holy and without blemish. So ought men to love their wives as their own bodies. He that loveth his wife loveth himself. For no man ever yet hated his own flesh; but nourisheth and cherisheth it, even as the Lord the church: For we are members of his body, of his flesh, and of his bones. For this cause shall a man leave his father and mother, and shall be joined unto his wife, and they two shall be one flesh. This is a great mystery: but I speak concerning Christ and the church. Nevertheless let every one of you in particular so love his wife even as himself…." (KJV)

When a man is done with something, he is done. It takes the love of God to cause a man to love his wife enough to hang in there especially when he is done. It is also humbling for a man to do something he doesn't want to do. I believe that is God's way of keeping men humble. A wife can be flighty. trying, nagging, testing, annoying, bossy, defiant, irritating, obnoxious, hormonal, temperamental, emotional, never really happy with her hair, nails and or body. We women also, as my brother would say, "have a monthly oil change." Men cannot relate and most men do not understand. Many husbands grow tired of these things, they no longer want to obey God and cover a multitude of faults in love. They choose to abandon and change their mind about loving their wives. Instead of exercising love that covers a multitude of faults or sin, they would simply rather not love. They look for greener grass. They would rather abandon to relieve themselves to get peace of mind or a piece of (I don't have to say it, do I?). A man that truly loves his wife will put up with his wife. A man that does not love his wife will abandon her.

A man needs the character of God to deal with a woman. Men don't think that we ride on the short bus; men think that we are just plumb crazy; they think we should be committed and not even have the privilege of riding on the short bus. It takes strength, conviction and the heart of God for a man not to give up on his wife. They disregard ***Ephesians 5:25-33***. Consequently, many men do not know how to value love and loyalty. Unless they are helped, they do not know how to seek out the resources that will help them work in love and harmony with their wives.

Men who get the resources and strength to hang in there are happier and their lives are filled with quality, virtue and honor amongst their family and friends overall. I encourage every husband not to quit on his wife. I encourage you to seek the Lord in handling her with the obedience of loving her. God created us women. He knows all of the codes on how to love and cherish us. He will give to every husband the combination. God will also send reinforcements to help men when things can get a little overwhelming. God will also refresh you with methods and events that will keep your engine going. When a wife is charged by her husband's love, unless she is a spawn of Satan, she will honor, respect and reverence her husband.

Being obedient is not bad, but it can feel like that sometimes. The great thing about being obedient, is that it's so rewarding and fruitful. ***Deuteronomy 28:1-6*** reveals in today's terminology, when we are obedient to His word, our relationships will be blessed, our homes will be blessed, our refrigerators and pantries will be full, our children will be blessed, our land will be blessed, our businesses will be blessed, whatever we put our hands to will be blessed, wherever we plant our feet is blessed, our cars will be blessed, and our jobs will be blessed. All we have to do is have faith that God's word is true, and obey. **Pray** and ask God to help you in every area of your life to be obedient to what is right. Ask God to help you not make excuses so that your life does not turn into a big excuse.

~ Joy While Experiencing Tribulation ~

We never want or expect tribulation. The older I get, the more I have come to realize that everyone experiences tribulation via death, sickness, trauma, extreme circumstances and/or some horrible tragedy at one time or another. It is not a mystery, we are informed by God in His word that we will have tribulation. Quite naturally, some of us do not handle those times very well. We all see that tribulation knocks on every one's door. But when it shows up at our door step for visitation, we question, *Why and why me?* We think tribulation should not happen to good people. We get angry with God. We feel sorry for ourselves. We question God's love, power and existence. How can we be joy, when the moments of tribulation can be so vexing?

To be joy during tribulation is to live by the six important truths underlined below:

Do you remember a few chapters back, one of the definitions of joy is "happy" and one of the definitions of happy is "willing"?

The first step forward in being joy during times of tribulation: **We must be *willing*** (see p. 36) **to be joy**. Our misfortunes will provoke certain emotions that are the opposite of joy. Our willingness plays an important part in not cooperating with those provoked emotions. Being joy will help us to see that our emotions of fear, depression, suppression, grief, misery and such will not change anything but the quality of our living. If we think about it, tribulation is bad enough as it is. Why should we let our tribulations consume our thoughts and ultimately our entire lives? The overcoming power of Christ in us gives us the ability to deal with our tribulation while enjoying all the other aspects of our lives. My daughter went full-term with her baby. However, some very unfortunate things happened at the hospital, and my grand baby Elijah passed away. It was heart wrenching and tragic. Some days afterward, I was complimenting my daughter on how well she was handling the matter, and she said, "Mom, I do not have a choice." She was **willing** to be joy because she did not want to be miserable. Jesus said in ***John 16:33*** (KJV), "These things I have spoken to you, that in Me you may have peace. In the world you will have tribulation; but be of good cheer, I have overcome the world." I thank God that in Christ I can have peace while going through hardship and in Him I will overcome.

I also thank God for being a very present help in the time of trouble. ***(Psalms 46:11)*** Now think with me. If Christ is a very present help, then His joy is very present as well. This leads me to the second step: **We must stir up the joy of the Lord in us**. This is how we can be of good cheer. Stirring up the joy of the Lord in us involves thinking on things that will cause us to rejoice. Dr. Siegel has labeled this ability as, "Mindsight (to see the internal working of our minds) it helps us get ourselves off of the autopilot of ingrained behavior."

The third step: **We must remember that we can take ourselves off of the autopilot of misery, grief, fear, depression, suppression, heartache and such like to be joy**. God allows tribulation in our lives for a purpose even if that purpose might be to keep us in relationship with Him. It is a wonderful thing to be in relationship with our Lord and be able to get His mind about what we are going through. Bishop Howard Calvin Ray made a powerful statement while ministering at a Prophetic conference that I was attending. He said so eloquently, "There is nothing that we are going through and nothing that we have been through that God has not graced us to be able to handle, if we perceive His mind."

The fourth step: **We must tap into the mind of God during our tribulation.** The mind of God is an awesome place. It is also the place that we flow in His grace (divine ability). God loves to communicate with us. He takes pleasure in directing us. This is the beauty and benefit of being in relationship with Him. The mind of God can be explored through:

** Reading the *Bible*
** God speaking directly to us through prayer, supernatural visitation and through a prophetic vessel.
** Teaching/ preaching of His word.

If we do not pray, read, or hear teaching/preaching it will be difficult knowing His mind and also recognizing when He speaks to us.

During times of tribulation, quite naturally our attention is on our misfortunes. However, shifting our attention to how much we love God proves to be most effective. You might ask, "Why should we focus on our love for God when tribulation causes us to wonder about God's love for us?" The reason is because of a promise God made to us. ***Romans 8:28*** (KJV) says, "All things work together for good to them that love the Lord and are called according to his purpose."

The fifth step: **We must remember that all things will work together for our good because we love Him.** This promise is ours with no expiration date.

Psalms126:5 depicts that with God we may sow tears but we will reap joy. In the mind of God, our tears won't last. They will only be from a span of night to day. ***(Psalm 30:5)*** We must not allow our minds to dwell on the horrible or painful details of our experiences. Maturity helps us to accept that tribulation happens. We understand that we do not like it, but God's grace helps us to move on. Constantly thinking on our painful experiences will consume us and deter us from being on course with our divine purpose. Thinking on those things will also cause us to relive the tragedy or pain over and over and over again. God does not want us reliving pain and suffering. The times I have cried the most have been when I would not stop reflecting on the harsh things that had happened. I just wouldn't let it go. God wants us to be glad and rejoice when we are blessed to see another day. ***Psalms 118:24*** (KJV) says, "This is the day which the Lord hath made; we will rejoice and be glad in it."

We must not feel obligated to keep unfortunate memories alive, especially those that concern loved ones. We are not turning our backs on our loved ones when we stop reliving their tragedies. The memory of the loved one is not the tragedy, and our loved ones would not want us dwelling on their deaths. They would want us to remember what they shared with us, their lives, their legacies. Going to the land of a sea of graves and stopping to kneel at a cold tombstone will only remind you of the harsh reality of death not the beauty of living. God never instructed us to do that. However, He does instruct us to set up memorials of Him delivering His people for generation to generation. (***Exodus17:14*** and ***30:16***).

If we can think about the unfortunate things that happens over and over again, we can do the sixth step: **To be joy, we must remember that our Lord who is multi-faceted will deliver us over and over again from the multiple tribulations we face.** God is our fortress, deliverer, help in the time of need, giver of abundant life, Prince of

Peace, healer, restorer, provider, protector. God is the Alpha and Omega. God is Omnipotent, Omnipresent and Omniscience. Our tribulation will never be greater than He.

When we set up our life with things to help us to remember the following important steps, our tribulations will not consume our lives. We must:

1. **Be *willing* to be joy**
2. **Stir up the joy of the Lord in us**
3. **Take ourselves off of the autopilot of misery, grief, fear, depression, suppression, heart ache and such like to be joy.**
4. **Tap into the mind of God during our tribulation.**
5. **Remember that all things will work together for our good because we love Him.**
6. **Remember that our multi-faceted Lord will deliver us over and over again**

When we don't do these things, our tribulations will be prolonged and sometimes even fatal. I had a neighbor who grieved herself to death after mourning the death of her sister. Being grievous can literally take our lives. One day a repeat customer came to see me. Since I had last seen him, he had lost weight and hair as a result of chemotherapy. He seemed down. He was considering ending his treatments because for quite some time the quality of his living had been diminished to three weeks of being sick which confined him to his bed and one week of partially feeling better. He came to see me because he wanted a new car before he died. He wanted to scratch it off his bucket list. I told him, "Let's get all the information (that I needed) and see what we can do."

While setting up his deal, I asked him how his friend was doing. He then shared with me with tears in his eyes that she was dying of Crohn's disease, cirrhosis of the liver and sugar diabetes. She had little time left. As he cried, he stated that he hated going to see her because he would feel like it might be his last time seeing her. I encouraged him to turn that around. I told him, "Love going to see her because it might be your last time. Do not consume yourself with negativity. Let your last days with her be joyous, enjoy every last moment you have with her and make good memories." When I shared those words with him, he took my advice, stopped crying and enjoyed his remaining time with me. He was a recording artist and in his new car we sat and listened to his music recordings of the good that he had done in his life. I sent him away with some excerpts of this book for him and her. It had not been published yet but I felt the urgency to give it. He later told me that their visits together were so much better. She loved the new car. They went on outings and enjoyed themselves. As a twist of fate, that time of enjoying her was for him. She buried him six months later.

Our bodies are not designed to house a deluge of negative emotions. Therefore, rather than bottling up these feelings, we should give them to the Lord the Lord and live like we only have today. Jesus Christ came so that He can bear our infirmities. He came to take the whole weight of the world on his shoulders. He is a "Big Boy"; His purpose for coming to earth is to handle it. Our privilege is to turn it over to him to handle. The Lord wants us to realize that even in the midst of our storms we can have perfect peace in Him. I am a living witness. I have experienced many tribulations causing me much pain. My pain rode to town on the train of my loved ones dying, sicknesses, trauma, lies, tragedies, betrayal, neglect and abuse. While it is true that some people experience more pain than others, we all have a story to tell. Yet, I can attest to the fact that the Lord will carry our load and us when we call on Him, much like implied in the well-known *Footprints* poem. When we no longer have the strength to go on, His strength gives us the ability to keep moving forward. I have compiled some life-changing events that were harsh realities. I share with you the challenging details of the tribulation leading up to the triumph. My prayer is that something mentioned in these testimonies will find you and encourage your heart as you triumph through your tribulations.

TESTIMONIES 1-2

(Joy While Experiencing Sickness & Death)

I remember talking to my mother on the phone and got an alarming perception that something was wrong. My mother was talking to me like all was well but the feeling that something was wrong did not go away. I then went to see her. When I saw my mother her skin was a grayish tone. I asked about the last time she had seen her doctor. She defensively denied a need to see her physician. After that visit, I continued to pray and begged my mom to go to the doctor. She still refused. Even with all of my praying, the deep concern I felt did not go away. Eventually, because of the push of my ex-husband, she went to the doctor. The doctor's report was that she had diabetes and hypertension.

A few weeks later, my mother ended up in the hospital from collapsing. While in the hospital, to our surprise the doctor reported that she had advanced stages of breast cancer. I watched my mother quickly go from a beautiful woman to a weak, balding, helpless woman. She could no longer walk and eventually lost her mental faculties because the cancer invaded her brain. As I would walk in her room, tears would stream down her face as if she still had some consciousness but was trapped in a body that would no longer cooperate with her.

The doctor pulled my brother and me aside to tell us that our mother only had a short time to live. He also told us that they were going to stop feeding her because it was a matter of time before she would die. I asked him if he was saying that they are going to allow her to starve to death? He said yes, there was nothing else they could do. I believed that my mother was going to live, regardless of what they said, so I instructed them to put her on a feeding tube. I did not want to work against God as I believed that He was going to heal her body from those diseases. My thoughts were, "Why should I allow them to starve her to death?" I must tell you, seeing my mother's health deteriorate was not easy. However, I did whatever I could do to make her comfortable. I prayed and believed God until the end that she was going to pull through.

I remember after leaving my mother's hospital room I would cry in the elevator many times. However, by the time I reached the car, I stopped crying. I would begin to meditate on what I believed. In my heart I fully believed God was going to restore my mom. I was certain that my mom was going to conquer this and live the victory of a happy disease free life. To me, the experience was merely temporary. I held onto ***Psalms 30:5***, which states I may cry for a few minutes but joy was going to come quickly. Despite my faith and heart's desire, my mother's journey on this earth ended. I believed so strongly that she was going to be with us a little longer. Did I have faith? Yes, I did. I did not waiver. However, I have learned in life that some things are greater than what we believe.

There are a number of reasons why what we believe and hope do not come to fruition. For one, sometimes the things that we believe and hope are not the will of God. What we believe may be a good thing and our intentions may be good, but it still may not be the perfect will of God. Remember our ways and thoughts are not like His. ***(Isaiah 55:8)*** Many times our beliefs are motivated by our selfish desires. Secondly, there are times that we need more than our mere belief. We need the power gifts (Working of Miracles, Gift of Faith and Gifts of Healing) to bring forth miracles. There are times that we need to set ourselves aside for fasting and praying in order for healing or a miracle to take place. Thirdly, there are times that we need the revelation gifts of the Holy Spirit to reveal how to fix the problem.

Even when we do not get our prayers answered in the ways we want them to be answered, we must still count it all joy. We should never forget that we are in His love, regardless of any situation. We must seek God for the answers and trust that He is still in control. He said, "I have overcome the world." I sincerely believe that my mom is in heaven. She is doing better than all of us. I know that she will live forever. She is no longer suffering because of illness or from an emotionally abusive husband. On the contrary, she is enjoying a disease-free life, which was an answer to one of my prayers. When I attended my mother's home-going, I was able to laugh and sing without grief. To this day, every time the temptation of sadness tries to come, I just remember that she is with God. She is doing much better than I am and that puts the biggest smile on my face.

The death of a loved one is not an easy thing to face. It certainly is one of the harshest realities of life. It is something we all must face and accept that it is going to happen. We are even appointed to die. We too will leave an empty space in someone's heart when we go. It is up to each of us to make the best of the life we are given even when death is part of it. Each day that we live, we should love the people that God has given us to love. Joseph and April Helton demonstrated that type love for each other every day. They had the storybook picture-perfect relationship that people dream of having. April, at age twenty-seven, was diagnosed with a thyroid disease. The doctors scheduled her two weeks out to get more testing and treatment. Unfortunately, she did not make it through two weeks. She died quickly and unexpectedly. It was a shock to all who knew her. She was a beautiful, blonde-haired, blue-eyed, pretty woman with a petite, very lean and fit physique. She was charismatic and full of life. Her death was a loss for many.

Her husband, I believe, felt the loss the most. However, still feeling the sting of her death, he focused on the joy of knowing her. He said that there were two things she loved for him to do and they were "her and music." We laughed together when he said that. He is moving forward now by writing music. He said that being negative will not help anything. He has to make his mark in life that is what she would want. He gave me permission to share a portion of two incomplete songs that he has started writing for her.

<u>Song One</u>

"Did I fall asleep in Heaven? Could this be a dream?
To wake up just beside you would be the sweetest thing.
I thought I knew forever, now not sure what that means.
My questions go unanswered even in my dreams."

They were scheduled to take a trip to Hawaii shortly after her unexpected death to spend some time with our friend Sean who lives there. They had everything mapped out, thanks to April. She wanted to ride motorbikes along the coast. (He still planned to go to Hawaii and take her ashes with him so she can ride along.) After the trip, they were planning to have a baby. Even with being in touch with that reality, his heart is filled with gratitude for the precious time that he spent with her.

<u>Song Two</u>

"How does one follow up the finest feast
but to cleanse the mouth with water.
My time was truly enjoyed April.
What can I say but thank you.
Thank you for the knowledge you provided me.
To know my soul mate, to dream of what was once absolute reality
My heart beats as my soul weeps."

"Live, Love, & Inspire." (Joseph Helton)

Joy is a key ingredient that makes life worth living after the death of a loved one. Live life to the fullest. Every minute is precious and valuable. Make the best of it. Once it is gone, it is gone forever. Do not waste your life. Give of yourself, love, share, laugh and laugh some more. Please do not allow tribulations to change you in a way that you no longer enjoy life or even want to live. That would be such a waste. If someone passes, cherish their memory, enjoy their legacy but sojourn where life is flourishing and *live*!

TESTIMONY 3

(Joy While Experiencing Living a Lie)

After my mother's home-going, we went to the church for her repast. My brother told me that he wanted me to meet someone. He introduced me to an aunt who was the sister of a man that I didn't know. I had heard of him. By introducing me to her, he was implying without saying that her brother was my father. My mother was not in her grave for an hour and my brother was giving me information that I could not validate with my mom. I did not like my brother's timing. I also felt that the gesture was disrespectful to our mother. Years before my mother died, I was nineteen and engaged to be married. A man came to our home and he and my mom went down to the kitchen of her split-level home. She told me to go up to my room. This seemed strange because my mother never sent me to my room when we had visitors.

When the man left, a sense of gloom hung in the house. It seemed very strange. I wanted to know why the man came to our home. My mom said he wanted to know if he was my father. I could not believe it! Of course I began asking questions. Yet the answer that ended our conversation was "No, he is not your father. I ought to know who your father is!" Eighteen years later my mom went home to be with the Lord. I was thirty-seven. A month after my mother's funeral, one of my neighbors, who was also my ex-husband's mother's friend, wanted to help our girls financially to go on a mission's trip to Brazil. He also stated that he knew someone who desired to contribute as well. I was told to call him. I didn't know that the someone who wanted to help my girls was my biological father, and the neighbor was married to my biological father's sister. All those years, I did not know my aunt lived a few doors down from me and my ex-husband's mother's friend was my uncle. The day came for me to call, in my mind, a kind man that wanted to help my daughters. When I called him, he never revealed to me that he was my father. He talked about how pretty my singing was at my mother's funeral, me having a music career and mostly about how much he loved all of his children. He started naming them and what they were doing career-wise. I wondered, "Why is he constantly saying he loved all of his children?"

When I hung up the phone I had overwhelming feelings that the man with whom I had spoken was my father. I was immediately flooded with mixed emotions. I cried, felt annoyed, anger and doubt. I remembered what my mom said to me. God then spoke to me and said, "That man can be your father 99.9%, and if you do not allow him to make it right, it will be because of strife, contention, and an unforgiving heart. This revelation was heart wrenching. I cried and cried in my office. I was hoping that no one came to the office because I was a mess. What hurt the most is that I did not have my mother to ask, "Why?"

That information was both shocking and incredible. All of the questions that I ever asked about myself that were really never answered . . . were answered in that single moment. I had to deal with being lied to when I trusted every word that came out of my mom's mouth. This discovery meant that much of my childhood was riddled with lies. That is a terrible feeling. I wondered why I had to live a life void of such an important truth. Why did I have to believe a man was my father, one who truly was not? Adding to the puzzle, I was told to believe it about a man who did not raise me. Daddy accepted me as his daughter. I am his "Rob Rob." However, because he and Mom were not together I rarely saw him. Daddy's mother disowned me. I grew up watching her shower my sister with gifts, love and affection, but she had nothing for me.

Emotionally this event could have taken me down for days, but, I chose to see the good in all of it. ***Psalm 37:23*** (KJV) says, “The steps of a good man are ordered by the LORD, and He delights in his way.” I was faced with accepting the fact that my mom was gone and could not answer my questions. I had to get a grip on myself just to handle my pressing responsibilities. I embraced trusting and believing that God was going to guide me on this new path. No one that evening or in the days that followed knew the emotional trial I was experiencing. The outcome of this testimony resulted in the Lord seeing me through. I did not act out. There was no hit list for all of my family members who knew all of these years and did not tell me, especially during those times, that I needed a father the most.

Instead, forgiveness was granted to every one of them. They watched me as a welfare recipient, knowing that my father owned his own trucking business. He lived in a beautiful suburban home built from the ground up, while I lived in the ghetto and walked to school with a hole in my shoe. There was a time that I had to wait until the first of the month to get new shoes. In addition, I had to forgive him for raising his other children, giving them all they needed including the emotional and moral support that only a father can give, all the while excluding me. I could not be envious. I did not hate my mom for lying to me, nor did I allow deception to cloud my emotions. I refused to walk around like a victim, choosing instead to walk and see myself as being victorious. I chose to walk in joy and look at the positive purpose in all of this.

Today, my father and I have a wonderful, close relationship along with my five half brothers and sister, Vitaleese. She is a moral support to me and I to her. My brother Tim has been there for me when I was left alone forced to deal with some of the harsh things I faced during the unfavorable situations involving my ex-husband. He also would school me about men when I became single. My brother June is my movie buddy; no matter when I am coming to town, June is taking me to the movies. Stevie is my prayer partner. He also gives me a good kick in the pants from to time to time to do better in life. He has the attitude that most military personnel and athletes have. They have been stretched and taken beyond the struggle of pain and challenges. My brother Steve played in the NFL for years. He will not allow me to have a lazy, sniveling mindset. Ron is the baby brother, my comedian and encourager. That guy has brought me so much joy and encouragement through the good times and the bad. Milton is the oldest and lives in another state. I have only had a few times with him. It is without dispute, he is my blood. It is good every time I see him.

I thank God I was not robbed of the chance to be in relationship with my brothers and sister. When we gather together, we always have a good time. We cut up and laugh like family should. There is no trying to make up for the past. I know that is fruitless. I wholeheartedly believe that my mother and father holding back the truth wasn't because they didn't love me. I always knew that my mother loved me and I know now that my father loves me. At the end of the day, that is what matters most.

In the scheme of life, we may not understand God's timing. We may not like God's timing. We may have questions like, "Why couldn't God move in my favor at this time or that time?" We may think or say, "It would have been so much better if God would have done a particular thing at this time or that time." If we could, we would make our lives so easy, comfortable . . . without pain, trials and tribulation.

But if everything went our way, we would end up being ungrateful, haughty creatures.

If it never rained, we would not appreciate the sunshine. If we never felt pain, we would take for granted feeling good. If we did not have trials and tribulation, we would never be humbled to need a living God.

God has given us everything that we need to live a quality, joyous life. The things that we go through are often uncomfortable and unfortunate but necessary because it prevents us from being lazy, spoiled, ungrateful and Godless.

TESTIMONY 4

(Joy While Living with a Debilitating Disease)

I was watching a church service on TV. The minister of the hour was talking to a man whose stance was abnormal. It was very obvious that he was physically impaired. His body was twisted and very thin. The minister asked the man what was wrong with him. The man stated that he had a disease that changes his muscle to bone (fibropysplasi ossificans progressiva). I thought, *Oh my God, I have never heard of such a thing*. He said the disease caused him tremendous pain and it felt like someone was twisting his bones every minute of the day. His speech was slurred as if the muscles in his cheeks and tongue had started to turn to bone. The minister asked him if he could still thank God in his condition. In his twisted disposition, the man said, "Yes." The minister said to him, "Tell us how." The man began elaborating on why he was so thankful. He thanked God that he still had the mobility of his legs to walk. He thanked God that he opened his eyes and saw another day. He thanked God for having his right mind. With his pale complexion and his contorted body causing his head to be twisted in an upward position, he thanked God for planting the stars in the sky for him to see. I just cried when he said those words. He touched my heart deeply. He literally appreciated things that we take for granted every day.

After he listed the many things that he was grateful for, with his crackly, dry-sounding voice he sang the song *I Can Only Imagine* by

Mercyme. He sang of the glorious time of what it could be like to walk with the Lord, to look upon his face, wondering if his heart would sing or if he would be so awestruck that he could only stand -- or perhaps kneel -- in silence. Would he sing praises or would he even be able to speak. As the title says, he could only imagine.

I was deeply touched as that man sang. He did not have a singing voice, but his singing was beautiful. It was beautiful because he sang with true conviction. He sang with the revelation of being in the presence of a true and living God despite his circumstances. I could tell that the joy of Jesus still remained in him. This joy was a *source of power*, flowing from his heart through the veins of his existence regardless of his pain and suffering. His sickness did not penetrate his joy. He had ***Urban Joy***. I was so moved by that man's testimony. My trials seemed even more insignificant, and I immediately began to thank God for everything that came to my mind.

TESTIMONY 5

(Joy While Experiencing Being Struck Down)

A tall, distinguished man was walking on our lot, checking out our inventory. I went out to welcome him as well as assist him. We talked as we walked. He told me what his intentions were for coming to our lot. He was curious to see if we could help him. I assured him that we could and proceeded with working a deal with him. While working, we also were getting to know a little more about each other. He told me how he had been saved since he was seven years old. He had a glow about him as he talked. He proceeded to tell me about the day his life changed forever. He was 48 years old and owned a lawn care business. As he told me his story all I could do was put my hand over my mouth as my eyes stretched open in unbelief. He wrote out his testimony. Please hold onto to your seat as he gives in detail his traumatic experience.

"October 12, 2000, at 8:15 a.m., I was in a life-threatening accident. As I was standing on the edge of the roadway behind my lawn-care trailer which was hitched to my 2000 model Chevy truck, I was struck by a 1985 Dodge van. In a standing position between the two vehicles, the van was crushing me as it continued to go forward rolling me from side to side. The bumper of the van started to go under the bottom of my trailer. I knew I was in great physical danger and would continue to be injured, if not killed. At this point I remember saying, 'God Help Me!'

"The front of the van went under my trailer with me on the front of it forcing me under my trailer. The van began to bounce apart from the trailer. I remember falling to the pavement. I knew that I was seriously injured. As I lay there on the pavement, I began to see all of the things lying near me about two feet from me. They were parts of my body. I saw my left boot with part of my leg sticking out of it with stringy like flesh hanging on the end of it. I looked at my leg and from about six inches below my left knee, it was gone. I saw a two-to-three inch section of my leg bone with absolutely no flesh on it. It was lying within four feet of my body. I realized I was in a big pool of my own blood and that it was getting worse. A severed artery was pumping out blood from my left leg that had been cut off.

"I laid there helpless on the edge of the road. I remember thinking, 'Oh no! I am crippled! I will be in a wheel chair if I live.' As I tried to move, I instantly felt and knew that something was wrong with my left side. (I found out later in the hospital that all of my ribs were either cracked or broken.) The palm of my hand was split open between the ring finger and little finger. My little finger was severed and hanging on to my mangled hand by a stringy piece of skin and it was mashed flat. I knew I needed to do something. No one was there to help me. (I found out later that the van driver went into a state of shock.) Still conscious, I grabbed my phone hooked to my belt and dialed 911. I told the operator my location and seriousness of my injuries. I then hit the memory key for my brother-in-law.

"I just laid back in the roadway between the two vehicles still by myself. I really started to feel the pain. All I could do is pray, 'God please don't let me die.' Over and over again. Suddenly a man appeared in my face and said, 'Sir, are you a Christian, have you been born again?' I said, 'Yes, I am a Christian.' Then a lady appeared and took my belt and used it for a tourniquet on my leg to slow the bleeding artery. The man with her applied pressure to the bleeding artery to slow the bleeding all they could. They had to pump blood back into me because I almost bled to death. They rushed me to Gaston Memorial Hospital. They then rushed me twenty miles away to Carolinas Medical Center in Charlotte, NC. A six-member medical team worked on my leg and a six member team worked on my hand. It took them 6.5 hours to put me back together."

He now walks very well with a prosthetic leg. I would not have known if he had he not told me. In his testimony, he went on to explain how his suffering was tremendous physically and financially while recovering. He shared his reactions of questioning God and feeling sorry. But at the end of this traumatic ordeal, his heart is still serving the Lord. He is humbled and his will is to be joy. He wrote a testimonial for his wife, family, church and community that included a list entitled:

"My list of Thank-You's"

- I thank God for everything, first and most of all.
- I thank my wife for the love and sacrifice she made.
- I thank my family for their help, love and support.
- I thank the Doctors who helped me regain my life.
- I thank my Home Church for its exceptional support.
- I thank all the other churches that helped me, in many ways.
- I thank my many friends who helped me, in many ways.
- I thank my neighbors who helped me, in any way.
- I thank all the area business that helped me, in any way.
- I thank everyone who prayed a single prayer for me.

P.S. "I pray God's blessing on each and every one of you."
-- Albert Joe Mercer

TESTIMONY 6

(Joy While Experiencing Pain & Suffering)

I was at home recovering from one of the worst/best experiences in my life. I say worst because I had to get a hysterectomy. Tumors invaded my uterus. Up until then I had never had surgery, thus I was very nervous and uncomfortable about being cut open. I was very uneasy about parts being removed from my body that God created me to have. So I told God how I felt about the procedure, and I linked up with my friend Denise, who is an intercessor. Since she had gone through the procedure previously; she was able to keep me encouraged and to think right. During the operation preparation time, they constantly stuck me, trying to draw blood from my tiny veins, I began to feel overwhelmed. Although I tried to recall and focus on every encouraging thing said to me prior, I could not. The Lord knew that I was emotionally in trouble. He sent three intercessors, one of them being my daughter Angie, to encourage me before I had to go into the operating room.

The power of the believers banding together is awesome. When you are down, struggling, and trying to make it with all your strength and failing, the power of two or three coming together with you does indeed wallop an impact on whatever prevails against you. After the operation, I was not quite conscious; however, I felt tremendous pain. I felt like someone had cut up my intestine and just left me there to suffer. With all my strength, I slurred out, “Pain, please help me. Pain!” With blurred vision, I saw a nurse whose back was toward me. She replied, "I'm coming, hold on." The longer she took, the more I pleaded. The pain was so horrific that for the sake of my sanity, I cried out, slurring, "God, oh God, oh God." Eventually she administered pain medicine and I remember fading into unconsciousness. The operation called for me to get more than thirty-seven stitches. The tumors caused my bladder to deform, so the doctor had to put it back to its original state.

After the operation I could not laugh, cough, sneeze, or climb stairs for several weeks. One night I was drinking water and it went down my windpipe. My body automatically started coughing the water out. Each cough felt as if someone was digging my insides with a hot rake. I was very concerned that the hard coughing caused my stitches to undo, and the pain was tremendous. The first night home from the hospital, I was given a prescription. That medicine made my stomach so upset that I almost threw up. I knew I couldn’t throw up because it would also cause my stitches to undo. I was literally being held together by thirty-seven stitches. I could not take the medicine without a good amount of food in my stomach. Unfortunately, I did not have an appetite and eating made me nauseous. Four days I went without pain medicine because I did not have an appetite. Without the medicine, the pain was so severe that I passed out on the bed one night. I had three other close calls of passing out, however, I would just say *Jesus* and the symptoms of passing out would go away.

I am the type of person that loves to laugh, jump, dance, move about and have fun with people. For weeks I could not. I had to sleep with about ten pillows to make reclining a little less painful. I could not walk, sit, or lie down without feeling pain. I went through a good seven weeks of this ordeal until I found a way to laugh without using my abdomen. I could not help it. While I was in the hospital recovering and while I was home, I listened to a CD series by Pastor Joel Osteen called

Your Best Life Now. The message encouraged me to maintain my joy. Throughout the message Pastor Joel would encourage me to, "Be up on the inside."

There were so many times I felt like crying because of all my suffering. But God used Pastor Joel's CD to help me through it all. Laboring through this horrific time induced the birth of ***Urban Joy***. Going through the severity of pain that I went through, God revealed to me that joy can govern my entire being. Joy is my source of strength through it all. Within those seven weeks of recovering, everyone who came to see me or saw me at church, testified that I glowed and had nothing but joy. That really encouraged me even more.

I pray that the testimonies mentioned can help others in their darkest hours. ***Revelation 12:11*** reveals that sharing our testimony has a powerful, overcoming effect. I believe that none of us are put here on this earth to be selfish. We all have a responsibility to each other. We can help each other be joy by sharing the things that we have gone through and how we got through them.

I have not personally gone through this but many of my people in the United States have been enslaved, raped, brutally beaten, sodomized, dismembered, murdered/hung on a tree, separated from family members, treated less than human, spit on, had their homes burnt down and held back in every productive area. We as a people have found God. We have forgiven and now my race and the world has celebrated the first black President of the United States. Whether or not we agree with his administration, that alone is a triumphant story to tell and anyone who hears it should gain strength to keep moving forward.

Contradicting as this might sound, experiencing bad things can be good for us. Tribulations are humbling, causing us to draw closer to God and each other, and ultimately we live a more joyful, victorious life

~ *How One Can* Be Joy *with A Cheating Mate* ~

If you have suffered the unfortunate revelation of being cheated on by your mate, please grant me permission to take you on a journey back in time. Allow your imagination to see the events in your mind as I tell you a story about you. As the day approaches, the sun rises, blood still flows warm through your veins and the digital clock is precise with the time of day. Within the time of day, your mate is with someone else. Ironically, nothing stopped. Time kept moving forward during and after your mate got pleasure with spending intimate time with someone else. The satellites still orbited around the earth. Traffic continued to flow north and south down the interstate. The heart monitor still recorded the rhythm and beat of the patient's heart. Children laughed and frolicked in the playground. You were inhaling and exhaling as you continued to breathe. Unaware of the cheating, you were sleeping, eating, laughing, watching television, working, helping the children, and/or hanging out with friends.

The point is, during the act of cheating simultaneously you were functioning normally. Outside of the presence of your spouse, you single-handedly were moving forward. You calculated in your mind the next step that would be beneficial for you, your family and/or career. You were moving forward as if the act of cheating was not being committed. But in reality, it was happening. News flash! It was happening while you were moving forward. Not knowing about the cheating, you were going on with your life just fine. Your soul was freely living on. As harsh as the reality of an adulterous affair is, you must see that life goes on. You must make the best of your day. Clear your mind. Isolate the affair and set it aside. You must go on and enjoy the life that was given to you. Do not let the betrayal, disloyalty, unfaithfulness, etc., consume your life. They are not worth it. Your life is too valuable and precious to waste. Yes, your marriage contract was breached. But take it from a business woman, new contracts are written every day. It is not the end of your life, although it may feel like it. You have so many other things to live for and to be happy about.

As difficult as it might be to understand, disloyalty, betrayal and unfaithfulness are types of behavior embedded in the heart of mankind. T.D. Jakes said in his message entitled *The Secret Agents of Change*, "You don't always get to know when people change their mind about you." Jakes went on to explain that we will go on and behave like nothing has changed, but all the while it has. I would like to interject that we don't always get to know in advance that our spouse is going to be a cheater. We are not aware of the moment that the spark of love and affection exclusively for us has diverted to another. Many of us are caught off guard. We are going on with our life and suddenly, like a train wreck, we are hit with the reality that our spouse has changed his (or her) mind about the wedding vowels. Ironically, God knew that we would not keep His commandments and sent His Son to pardon us for our indiscretions. God knows that if things are not easy, convenient and or comfortable, the human race has proven to act without true consideration of the covenants and vows made to Him and to each other.

We live in a society in which we are always looking for something new, better, bigger, or greater, yet many times we do not respect or appreciate what we already have. Many don't uphold those things that have more meaning and depth such as loyalty, love, care, consideration, wholesomeness and faithfulness. Our morals and ethics are like sheets in the wind, flapping and flowing where ever the wind blows them. In life there are many temptations, dysfunctional circumstances, and immorality that corrode the fiber of honesty, loyalty and faithfulness. Unfortunately, that which is good becomes extinct. With the overwhelming evidence of acts of cheating from generation to generation, I now believe that for anyone to hope to commit to someone, it is the goodness, love and grace of God prevailing.

If your spouse has cheated, you must try to understand. We must find it in our heart to forgive daily. We must also realize that the minute that the cheating spouse asks God to forgive them, God will. We cannot set ourselves above God. To suggest something that might help your thought process, think about the wrong that you have done. Think about the times you were not honest, loyal and or faithful in other things. Just think about the justifications that you conjured up in your mind while committing the acts. Think about how your justifications made sense to you. God sees us diverting our love and affection away from Him daily. Try to understand how God feels when He sees us cheating on Him. Be reminded on how God has forgiven us for the numerous times that we have fallen short. In humility, maybe, just maybe, you might find it in your heart to forgive your cheating spouse.

Sometimes we can have this haughty, self-righteous attitude concerning certain sins. We develop this critical, stiff-necked attitude about the wrongdoing of others. I really love the account in the *Bible* when a group of people got together and threw this woman (who was caught committing adultery), at the feet of Jesus because they wanted her stoned to death. Jesus never gave them the courtesy of looking at them. He just kept writing in the sand. They were quoting scripture trying to judge this woman and Christ said, "He that is without sin, throw the first stone." Every last one of them must have known in their hearts that they were not perfect and had fallen short, because not one stone was thrown.

In order to be released from the emotional shackles of adultery, you must first have mercy and understanding that no one is perfect and we all have fallen short. You must also be void of pride. You must let go of the fact that your mate found pleasure in someone else. It is a harsh reality to come to know that we are not as special as we think we are in the heart of those we love. Mankind has a tendency to want to move on to something new, fresh, exhilarating and different to keep the lust of the eye and the pride of life going. However, all hope is not gone. I thank God that my worth is not determined by the lusts and preferences of others. Our hearts can be filled with the value of knowing that God will never leave us nor forsake us: we are always special to Him. "His thoughts towards us are precious." ***(Psalms 139:17)*** His precious thoughts towards us *never get old* and *He never* changes His mind about us. Who is greater and better than God?

It is pertinent that we do not let pride get the best of us. Pride, the same spirit that caused Lucifer to fall, will cause us to decline joy. Pride can escalate our emotions to the point of us wanting to kill our mates for choosing someone else over us. Pride will make us want to take vengeance. When I found myself having to deal with this situation in my life, I was very hurt and angry. I remained faithful to him; I was devoted only to him. In spite of the many temptations that came my way, I did not yield. I did not experience the pleasure of being gratified by another man for the twenty-six years of marriage, even when separated. Boy, oh boy, were there times that some gratification would have been wonderful! I was literally angry because I did the right thing.

My thoughts were, How dare he find pleasure in someone else and I didn't? How dare he breach our contract that we made to God and each other to appease his lusts and I didn't! I had to be true to myself that I was angry for some of the wrong reasons. I took my husband's betrayal very personally. I asked God to give me His heart of mercy and forgiveness because an adulterous affair is no "walk in the park" by any means.

Joyce Myers really helped me to be able to write about it with a right spirit. She said words to this effect, "Let God turn your pain into gain. Let God turn your mess into your message." She shared that it is not our burden of responsibility to keep secrets and be phony in order to preserve the integrity of those who violated us and caused us pain. Those words ministered to me. I realized that instead of internalizing my painful experiences, I can share them with hope that someone would gain wisdom, strength, stability, self-worth and the liberty of being joy. I realized that my story is my message. My prayer is that the details of my personal humiliations and sufferings to the victory of living ***Urban Joy*** may help someone get through this type hardship. My motive is not to expose but to implode the negative emotions that fester within because of this type hardship. My message is given from a position of triumph and victory, not defeat.

While my spouse was cheating, many disrespectful hurtful things were done intentionally and unintentionally. I experienced many phases in the midst of this trial such as the *Mask of A Good Samaritan, Convinced That It's Best, Just Friends, Another Agenda, Defrauding, Twilight Zone* and *Click Zone.* These phases involved one or all of the following: deception, disrespect, marriage boundaries being broken, self-indulgence without regard, dehumanization, disgrace, unsound judgment, defrauding and the lack of love. When there is infidelity, the signs may be obvious or obstructed. You may be going through similar phases, struggling to do the right thing. If you are, my prayer is that ***Urban Joy*** may strengthen and help you get through them successfully. I will share my struggles. I will expose my thoughts, gestures, prayers, reactions, and beliefs with hope that it will encourage Godly behavior, lighten the load of a heavy heart, prevent unnecessary pain and suffering as well as help preserve the sanctity of marriage. I will share my "Acceptance and Moving On" phase, which reveals the intimacy of my healing process. In sharing, my expectation is to guide many to get on the right course while dealing with this horrible truth. Now journey along with me as I expound on the phases that I experienced. My prayer is that the events and information written will enlighten, strengthen and promote right behavior.

Mask of a Good Samaritan

"We all wear masks, and the time comes when we cannot remove them without removing some of our own skin." -- Andre Berthiaume, Author/Assistant Professor. The *Mask of a Good Samaritan* phase is simply bad intentions masked by good deeds. A spouse doing good deeds for a specific person always in the absence of their mate may be masking something dark and hidden. If we are hiding adultery behind the *Mask of a Good Samaritan* we should be prepared that once it is removed, there is a possibility of removing our own flesh. ***Genesis 2:25*** (KJV) describes the marriage union as being one flesh. "Therefore shall a man leave his father and his mother, and shall cleave unto his wife: and they shall be one flesh." Throughout the record of time, adultery has been the number one reason why a marriage has been short-lived. Marriage certificates are annulled by a judge and the validity, virtue and value of the marriage becomes equivalent to a pile of ashes.

To prevent wearing the *Mask of a Good Samaritan* couples should nurture their marriage with honesty and avoid hiding behind deception. They should deem it important to be plugged into resources constantly upholding principles that will keep the marriage relationship healthy and working. Maintaining your marriage boundaries helps prevent separation and then divorce. Be careful of the repeated concentrated effort of going above and beyond being helpful to an individual, excluding your spouse. Set boundaries and maintain those boundaries. People will always have needs and we must use wisdom in aiding them. If your spouse refuses to wisely maintain those boundaries, something is wrong. You may be experiencing the phase of your spouse wearing the *Mask of A Good Samaritan.*

There was a woman in our church who was very needy. My husband, the pastor, felt compelled to minister to her every need, day in and day out. It did not matter the boundaries that he would break or the cost to achieve his mission. He had developed an unusually close relationship with her. He became so close, that he decided to put her on our *family* cell phone plan. He broke the boundaries of our marriage as well as our family by including this woman on our plan. His masked explanation, as the pastor, was that he was helping her because her phones were shut off. In the absence of bad motives, you and I both know that there are so many other good ways that she could have been helped. As his wife, I expressed my disapproval, however, he disregarded my disapproval and kept her on our family plan. Ultimately, he was able to talk with her privately anytime and anywhere, day or night without being charged.

Being so accessible to him, she was good to him. Secretly increasing talking with her resulted in him talking to me less and less. If I got a paragraph of conversation in a week from him, oddly in a bad situation, that was a good week. Unbeknownst to me, their relationship got even more personal. I discovered that he secretly called her by her middle name. When he was asleep, I seized the opportunity to check his call history. I counted at least eight times just that morning he talked to a female with an unfamiliar name. He awoke while I was looking at his phone. I asked him who was this woman that he had been spending so much time with on the phone. He was upset by my spying and grabbed his phone from me. He told me it was her, he just used her middle name. I thought, "No one ever called her by her middle name and I never heard him in public call her by that name." I said in many different ways that their relationship is a little too personal for a pastor and congregation member. After that incident, he would erase any call history before he went to sleep. I thought, "Why would a man who has nothing to hide do that?"

I would awaken wee hours of the night and hear him in the living room talking and laughing with someone on the phone. I always had a feeling it was her. One time I decided to confront him in the act. I quietly walked in on him. His eyes were big a saucers when he saw me. I asked him to whom was he talking during that time of night and he confirmed that it was her. We lived above her. His masked explanation was that she heard a noise and called him. *Really*? Three o'clock in the morning? The boundaries of our marriage were nowhere to be found. Their self-indulgence without regard to me had become their norm and my disgrace. Even without all the facts, I still knew something was wrong. As my dad would say, "I don't have to eat a whole cow to know that I am eating beef."

After almost two years of similar behavior, we separated. To interject the idiom, *"Where there is smoke there is fire."* I found the fire that was producing the smoke. Six months into our separation, I went to the phone company to take my name off of the Family Plan that she was still on. I got the phone records because "Einstein" did not calculate in his secret equation that I was the primary account holder. He never took into consideration that I had the authority to see all of his records stemming way back to when I was still living with him. They spent thousands of minutes every month on the phone together. He would call this woman as soon as he left our home to go to work. He spent the entire twenty-five-to-thirty-minute drive talking to her. He then called her when he was at work and talked from thirty minutes to an hour, three to four times throughout the eight hours that he worked every night. He would then talk to her on his way home twenty-five to thirty minutes more. He did this every day, week after week, month after month.

It felt like a dagger had gone straight into my heart when I looked at the month of December on my birthday and saw that he talked with her twenty-two times and called me zero times. I remember staring out of the window on my birthday hoping that he would call me or surprise me with something special. I got nothing and he did not call. What a waste of my time and emotion. Those twenty-two calls showed me he couldn't have cared less. It hurt deeply to see the reality of where his affections were. Unfortunately, my thinking that they were trying to put me together like a two-piece puzzle was true. Even when it is not in our favor, truth will always prevail. The truth was, my husband/pastor wore The *Mask of a Good Samaritan* to cover up his deception and how he changed his mind about me.

Convinced That it's Best

Convinced That It's Best phase is when a partner is flying solo and reckoning unsound reasoning and judgment as being sound and right. Be careful of the reasoning that will cause the sanctity of your marriage to crash. Marriage is a partnership that requires sound judgment especially during challenging times. If not careful, partners who single-handedly make decisions without the consent of the other partner could jeopardize the success and growth of the partnership. Do not allow the pressures of life destroy all that was done to build the partnership. ***Ecclesiastes 4:9-10*** (KJV) says, "Two are better than one; because they have a good reward for their labor. For if they fall, the one will lift up his fellow, but woe to him that is alone when he falls..." Woe to the partnership in which a partner in marriage insists on operating alone.

Our country was going through a gas crisis, so my husband and this same woman decided to go to work together. He verbalized that his reasoning was to save money. He thought it was best because they worked near each other. He knew that I, his partner, was not in agreement, but he proceeded with the plan despite my disapproval. I had no say as his wife. That was very humiliating, disrespectful and again our marriage boundaries were broken. The first day that they drove together, I was out doing my morning exercise and he came driving by with her lying prostrate in the passenger seat. My wonderful married pastor husband obviously saw nothing wrong with her lying beside him. He slowed her black PT Cruiser, which looked like a miniature hearse carrying the death of our marriage. She sat up, looking like a pale mortician and said, "Good Morning, Pastor Robin. Do you want a ride?" in an eerie joking way. My partner of twenty-four years never said, "Good morning." He muttered nothing out of his lips. He passed by me like road kill. We don't acknowledge road kill. I thought, "How in the world are you going to drive another woman's vehicle, while she is lying in an inappropriate position, while knowing I am not in agreement with your carpooling, and *you can't speak*?" OMG (Oh My Goodness), I was flabbergasted! However, I said, "No thank you," to her and turned away and continued to exercise.

Even bringing to his attention many times how his reasoning was disrespectful and a violation of our marriage boundaries, he did not break his stride. He continued with no regard. After they had ridden together several times, I met with her in his presence and told her how I felt about them riding together. I gave them the scripture not to let your good be evil spoken ***(Romans 14:16)*** and shun the very appearance of evil ***(I Thessalonians 5:22).*** I shared with her that he is her pastor and not her boyfriend. Our ministry training is that he is to have someone accompany him while ministering to the opposite sex. I told her that even Christ sent them out two-by-two and this practice is for her protection as well as his. I shared with her that I was not in agreement. I did not say anything to her. I said it to the man with whom I was in covenant. However, he had not respected my wishes so I came to her, woman-to-woman in his presence so nothing was misconstrued. After that episode, they stopped riding to work together but it did not stop them from going other places together alone while I was at work.

I had to suffer through the whisperings in our apartment complex that they were having an affair, the black pastor and a white woman. It was scandalous, juicy gossip quenching the thirst for a bunch of bored southern backwoods country folk looking for some action. One of our congregation members came to me wanting to know how to handle her neighbor reporting that she saw my husband and this woman in the hotel section of where we lived. I encouraged her to continue to allow the Holy Spirit to guide her and lead her and not gossip. The more people constantly saw them together alone, the more the rumors circulated in our neighborhood. This *Convinced That It's Best* phase caused a decrease in our church attendance, hurt our marriage more and caused an ungodly soul-tie to bond even tighter. Ironically, later his only explanation for filing for a divorce was, "I think it's best." Partners, if you want your marriage to work, be careful of making decisions without your partner. It could be a trap of the *Convinced That It's Best* phase that could utterly destroy your partnership.

Just Friends

Be careful of the *Just Friends* phase, which is simply having a friend that excludes the spouse. You and your spouse should share mutual feelings about your friends. All things done with your friends should be done out in the open with spousal consent. When married, friendships that involve secrets will never lead to any good. Your spouse may not hang out with you and your buddies, however, he or she should be in agreement with the actions of you and your buddies. Violating this principle can cause a marriage to function on one side. Functioning only on one side physically can be a sign that something is wrong. For instance, it could be a sign of being paralyzed from the effects of a stroke. It could be a birth defect. When married, functioning only on one side is spiritually unhealthy and could be a sign of a breakdown of marital ethics. God has graced married couples to work together as a team. When married, being on one accord about relationships with others is important. Come together and reason together for the purpose of agreement. Respect and consider each other's wishes. If your spouse is uncomfortable with your actions with a friend, don't force the friendship on your spouse. Slow things down with the friend and investigate the source of your spouse's discomfort. Remedy the discomfort by securing the sanctity of your marriage.

My husband's attentiveness to this woman was so constant that she openly called him her best friend. She gave him that title because he was always there for her. He stayed in her apartment for hours. He helped her with many things. He would fix things in her apartment; he showed her how to use the computer to pay her bills; he taught her how to drive a straight-stick drive. They did just about everything together without my consent, knowledge or permission. They walked to the mail box together just about every day. They went to stores together, they ate together, they went to the bank together, they went to the video store and picked out movies together. Wherever he went, it seemed that he found a reason to have her with him. With all his efforts and energy towards her, he stopped everything with me. We just coexisted. The only interest that he had to talk to me was about our young adult children and giving up my paycheck when I got paid.

Reflecting back, (before I got the phone records) I asked him to stop spending so much time in her apartment. She came to me several times saying that she and the pastor did not talk much anymore because I asked him to stop spending so much time in her apartment. The phone records revealed that they talked several times a day, many times more than an hour. Why did she hide that truth and lie? I would often call her and check on her with hopes that it would balance out her needing my husband so much. One day I had gotten an urge to call her. Her son answered the phone and said that she was in the living room with her pastor. I asked if I could speak with her. He put me on hold and when she got on the phone I greeted her and asked her what was she doing. She said looking at something on "Lifetime." Her son did not mention that he told me that my husband was there and neither did she mention it. We talked briefly. As she was hanging up, I told her to tell my husband that I said hello. She literally started stuttering and asked, "Do you want to talk with him?" I told her, "No, I called to check on you."

She called the next day and told me that when I called, they had just come back from getting ice cream together. He invited her out for ice cream. It was only just the two of them. She said that he wanted to show off his GPS system. I do not know why she felt compelled to call me the next day at work to tell me what they did. I could assume that it was conviction because she lied to me, or a cover-up for what they really did do, or she may have felt that she better tell me before someone else did. To this day, I am not sure why she called me. But of one thing I am certain: whatever it was, it wasn't right. When I ended the call, I could no longer concentrate. I left my job after she told me of their outing together and went home to address the matter. He didn't say why he did it. He just said that he was sorry. In tears, I told him that he was busted, not sorry. All of his actions with this woman, each time took a small part of me. But this deed took a big chunk out of me. Their ice-cream outing really bothered me because he had been defrauding me and not spending any time with me for quite some time. I shared with my husband that if I did such deeds with a man, it would be a major problem. I asked him why was it okay for him to continue to behave this way. He just stared at me. He had no words. I told him that I wasn't sure how much more of that type behavior I could take. Their *Just Friends* phase was looking more and more like *Friends With Benefits***.**

Another Agenda

Being married, be careful of having agendas that exclude your spouse. Married couples need quality time regardless of how little the time might be. Be careful of always putting people and other things before your spouse. It should be a given that your spouse is second to no one. Even though we have a profession or occupation that takes up most of our time, we should communicate in a way that our spouses should not feel slighted. With all diligence, we should respect each other's occupations, gifts, and talents; however, boundaries should be set concerning your time sanctioned for your spouse overlapping with another agenda. Keep the communication between the two of you uninterrupted. When things do overlap beyond your control, be considerate, communicate, and make up for the time taken.

My husband was consumed with helping this woman who seemed to always need him. Running to her rescue day in and day out to him was part of his job as a pastor. He stopped going out with us as a family, not to mention any type of quality time with me. I brought it to his attention countless times, thinking that it would prick his heart. His heart was pricked, but not in my favor. My daughters got on him about his behavior and questioned if he loved me. He never said that he didn't love me but he never said that he did, either. From their talks together, they decided that him taking me to the movies was a good idea. I remember being excited at work all day about our date to the movies. He was not home when I got there because he was with her. The girls and I did not talk about it. We all knew where he was, but we just chose to cheerfully talk about my date night. The sound of it was refreshing in our home.

When he finally came home, we had just a few minutes to catch the show. He hadn't seen or talked to me all day. Unfortunately, standing at the door he didn't see a need to greet me, either. He just made eye contact and said, "Are you ready?" with a blank expression on his face. I remember my heart sinking and feeling disappointed that he wasn't as excited as we were. I ignored what I saw, as usual, and said hello to him. I told him I was ready, just waiting for him. He didn't comment, he didn't wait for me nor escort me, he just turned away and headed down the stairs to get into his truck ahead of me. I said goodbye to the girls cheerfully, hoping that they did not get affected by his actions like I did. They were so happy for me that they were cheering me on as I walked out of the door. I needed that boost for what I was about to face.

He got in on the driver's side and sat there. He didn't open my door or help me climb into his truck. When driving, he didn't strike up one conversation. To break the ice, I told him that I bought him his favorite snacks for the movie. He didn't even say thank you. When I questioned him, he said, "Don't start it with me." I told him that I wasn't starting anything, I just knew that if someone says that they got you something thank you or no thank you should be the response. He then replied, "I'm not hungry." I remember thinking *wow*! I changed the subject by trying to talk about something happy. It was as if I was talking to the windshield. He was cold and distant. I asked if he was tired or not feeling well. He said, "I'm fine" with a glazed look in his eyes. Feeling low at that point, I shared with him that if he wasn't up to going, we could do it some other time. I tried to gracefully bow out. His response was that he was going because he was doing it for me. I replied, "I thought the outing was for *us*." He insisted that he was taking me because that is what he had planned to do all day. He didn't say it like we were on a date. It was like a military assignment being carried out. Right then the Lord instructed me to leave the matter alone. I quieted myself and just looked out the window wondering why it had to be like that. For the entire ride, the only thing he said was, "What time does the movie start?" The vehicle was silent other than the hum of the engine and road noise. As we got closer to the movie theater he asked again, "What time does the movie start?" I thought it was strange that he would ask that question again; it was the only thing he had said on the entire ride. His asking twice appeared as if he had something else on his mind, another agenda that did not include us going to the movie.

When we got to the movie theater, we were a few minutes late. He let me out at the curb to purchase the tickets and then he drove off to park. I went to get the tickets and asked was the movie crowded, the ticket agent said, "Yes, but there are a few seats left." I told her because of the limited seating, I was going to wait to see if my husband would want to catch the next movie. I waited and waited and waited on that curb for the sum of twenty-and-some-odd minutes. The movie had begun. We were missing the movie. I felt like I was waiting for an hour. It was very busy that night and hormonal teens were out showing their true colors. Some were revving and screeching with their loud modified engines and exhausts. More and more I became concerned for him.

My concerned thoughts were, "He knew the time of when our movie started because his only conversation with me was the question, *What time does the movie start?* What would detain him? Something has to be wrong for him not to call or text me to tell me what was detaining him." I thought it was best to stay put and wait. But then I thought what if something happened to him and he couldn't call me. I started to go look for him; maybe he needed my help. As I stepped off the curb, I looked ahead and saw him walking towards the theater. I was relieved; however, as I continued to look, I also saw his other agenda. He was walking with the cell phone to his ear. Miraculously, he was smiling and talking. What a wonder to behold, he could talk and the cold distant blank expression that he had with me was gone. Whatever ailed him ailed him no more.

I perceived it had something to do with that woman. For the first time in my life, I felt heat streak down my neck, back, then down to my feet like I had been hit by lightning. His other agenda was more important than his wife standing on a curb for more than twenty minutes, missing the movie that he brought her to see. I felt dehumanized. I personally could not have done that to any human being. He had already showed no excitement about the outing and to make it even worse, he left me at the curb for over twenty minutes. I was done. Baked to perfection. Someone could have stuck a fork in me. As we walked toward each other, he quickly rep-*lied* and said it was an emergency. The emergency was that the woman's family member wanted her daughter to come to church. *You-gotta-be-kidding-me*! He stated that we could catch the next movie and asked me not to be angry. I immediately felt like I was not worth a text to give me heads-up about him being detained. I felt like his thoughts of me were less than human.

I asked him to take me home. I turned my head to look out the passenger window, as my tears streamed down my face. I prayed right then and asked God to help me. I felt overwhelmed with abuse and neglect.

When we got home, he had no concern for me. He stayed out in the breezeway talking and laughing with neighbors. My daughters were there to try and console me. They asked where their dad was. I could only say, "Outside." I felt sick to my stomach. It felt like I could not breathe. I got the keys and left my home. His disrespect, disregard, neglect and emotional abuse was suffocating me. I drove and drove, cried and exhaled until I found an open restaurant. He went looking for me after my daughters lit him like a Christmas tree. When he found me, he greeted me with a joke. Eventually, he said he was sorry and fell asleep in my face as I talked. I remember feeling nothing as I watched him nod. I was numb.

To all my married readers, beware of the *Another Agenda* phase; it is the ADD (Attention Deficit Disorder) of marriage. Beware of your time and attention scattered abroad, neglecting one of the most important relationships in your life. There is a cure for this disorder. It has always been there just waiting for us to discover. The cure of the ADD of marriage is a term I created which is the ACC (Attentive Care & Consideration) antidote. The ACC antidote will aid in keeping a marriage healthy as well as functioning properly. It prevents couples from falling into the *Another Agenda* phase. The ACC antidote focuses more on your significant other than deeds, functions, events and duties at hand. It infiltrates our intent in communicating the solution regarding a conflict with scheduling. It erases the past and addresses the now. The Attentive Care & Consideration (ACC) antidote protects, preserves and values the joy that presently flows in a relationship.

Defrauding

It is normal and healthy to make love to your spouse often. It is dysfunctional and abnormal to be married and not make love to your spouse regularly. Today there is no excuse. Regardless of your physical challenges, there are methods available to aid in having a healthy sex life. If your sex drive is low, there are safe supplements to boost your drive. If there is an erectile dysfunction, there are many solutions for that as well. Be careful of defrauding your spouse. It could lead to major problems in the marriage. God says in ***I Corinthians 7:5*** (NKJV)

"Do not deprive one another except with consent for a time, that you may give yourselves to fasting and prayer; and come together again so that Satan does not tempt you because of your lack of self-control." Defrauding could also be a sign that your spouse is being satisfied elsewhere.

During a span of almost two years, I watched how my husband's attention was consumed with this woman day and night. He literally lost the sense that he was married. On our first and only ministry trip in Florida, we rented a beach house with ocean view. As I was coming down the steps looking for him, the two of them were walking in off the balcony after watching the ocean and the sunset together. They were discussing how beautiful it was when I walked up on them. Another time I went looking for him, he was in her bedroom with the door closed "helping her." At that point, I didn't even pray. I just walked in and abruptly interrupted him. I was becoming very intolerant of his behavior. At times when she would call our home for me, I would hear him in another room intercepting the call, forcing her to let him help her. I would hear him repeat, "I can help you with lady things." I had many thoughts like, "What is the purpose of this control and obsession?" There was always a reason why he had to be with her.

He eventually stopped all intimacy with me. I wondered how a vibrant man can go without sex as long as he appeared to have gone without. However, I did not notice a coloration of blue on certain parts of his anatomy either. I'm just saying. His excuse for not touching me was that we were having problems. However, he made it clear that he was not going to participate with any form of marriage counseling. He knew that he was going to be checked and he did not want that. I am here to tell you that it is tougher to be married and deprived. When you are single and not getting any is completely different than when you are married and not getting good loving. It can be likened to a person dying of starvation trapped in a room with food and forbidden to eat. Deprivation is violating one of God's spiritual principle. ***I Corinthians 7:4*** (KJV) says, "The wife does not have authority over her own body, but the husband does. Likewise the husband does not have authority over his own body, but the wife does." God said that his body belonged to me, but he violated that principle.

Sexual deprivation when married is torturous in more than one way. As an attractive woman, I would be hit on by co-workers and clients constantly. Only by the grace of God my strong convictions sustained me. I am a vibrant, healthy woman, even more so during that time. It was very challenging to stay kept. One of my former managers was tall, handsome, dressed nice, smelled good all of the time and was in good shape. This man always seemed to hug my shoulder right at a time when I felt rejected the most by my husband. He had a great sense of humor. He kept me laughing. He would always say just the right compliment to make me feel good as a woman. Although the man never propositioned me, I could tell that he was attracted to me and his attention started to get to me.

Neglected so long by my husband, my self-esteem had started to crumble. My need to be touched was getting stronger and stronger. I felt like Marvin Gaye, in need of "Sexual Healing." One day those feelings were so strong my emotional stability was leaving me. When he walked by me, I could have sung, "B-a-a-a-aby I'm hot just like an oven. I need some lovin'." I wanted to jump his bones. My thoughts were bad, which made me feel bad. I went into a private restroom at my job and cried until I travailed to God. While praying, I asked God to deliver me from the thoughts of being with that man. I said to God. "I know you said, 'Let us lay aside every weight, and the sin which doth so easily beset us.' ***(I Corinthians 12:1)*** However, I am so weak I cannot stop feeling this way. If you do not take your mighty hand and move, I am going to have that man with a capital HAVE." I knew that God did not bring me this far to be up to no good regardless of how I was being treated. God helped me. Without notice, the co-worker was transferred within that week.

Defrauding your spouse is a mean, ugly, torturous thing to do. If you are having issues, get help before it is too late. Get the help you need to get out of the "Defrauding Phase" so that your spouse is not tempted to do something that he or she really doesn't want to do. Do not wait month after month thinking that your spouse is okay with being starved. If your spouse is vibrant, trust me, he or she is not okay. Something is wrong with that, and your partner may be tempted to go elsewhere if you are not consenting. You can push a person only so far. Eventually the right buttons are going to be pushed. We are human, not God. We do not have self-control twenty-four hours a day and seven days a week no matter how hard we try. We have been engineered to procreate. Our bodies are wired and geared to have sex automatically. We have nothing to do with how we were created. However, we have all to do with how we control ourselves. We also have all to do with doing right by not defrauding our spouses.

Twilight Zone

There are many twists and turns that happens in life. We must be careful of them causing us to enter into the space and time of the "Twilight Zone." *The Twilight Zone* was a television program that captured a world of escapism and adult drama. It is a zone that brings to life a physiological twist of reality. When married, this phase of twisted reality is the horror of wrong being right in full-fledged drama. If not careful, this phase can be the downfall of a marriage. As a pastor's wife, many times I had to suffer through a religious "Twilight Zone." It's a zone where the religious operate in an above-the-law mentality. Principles are violated and rules and boundaries are broken, as if heaven gave special permission. If you are married to a spouse in the ministry and find yourself in the religious "Twilight Zone," I pray for your deliverance. I pray that God will bring about a reckoning of truth.

On TV, *The Twilight Zone* had many episodes. Like on TV, I lived through many episodes, however, I will only mention four.

(Episode 1) During the dusk of a particular day, I went looking for my husband. I figured he would be with her. I walked to her apartment only to find her door cracked open and no one in the kitchen, which was unusual. As I entered, I said *hello* and got no answer. I walked straight down the hall to her bedroom, opened the door all the way and there he was. He was massaging her head as she was lying in her bed on her back in her sleepwear. The room was dark. I was about to say something, but when I heard him praying quietly, I said nothing. She suffered from migraines and I assumed that he was praying over her for that reason. I remember feeling weird seeing him touching her that way. So many thoughts went through my mind. As his wife, I tried to think positively. I hoped that he would rethink some of his actions. However, he repeated the same episode more than once despite any of my concerns.

(Episode 2) One warm summer night, I came home from work a little early. As I was walking to my apartment, my husband and this woman were just walking out of her apartment as she was handing him his lunch bag. They were close, laughing and talking without any reservation; they hadn't seen me yet. She was walking with him to his vehicle to see him off to work. This apparently had been a normal practice because they were very relaxed and comfortable. He had not seen or talked to me all day. Being in a mode of not talking to me, he looked at me as I was walking towards them but he never opened his mouth to speak. He just continued to laugh and talk with her as I walked past him. She said hello but he, the pastor, didn't speak. I said hello to him, and he then spoke. Oh, the thought of kicking him in his "ball-jangles" seemed so appealing! However, instead, I remember immediately praying to God to help me as I climbed the stairs. I felt like I was in a bad dream of witnessing my husband cheating on me in my face and I desperately wanted to wake up.

Unfortunately, even our Sunday morning services fell into the space and time of the *Twilight Zone*. I have witnessed the most eerie things in church. With all of the emotional, spiritual, social and moral instability she had in her life, he preferred her to pray at the altar alongside him. He actually had her laying hands on people. I remember feeling displaced as I stood on the sidelines watching all the years of our ministry training hold no validity. All of our ministry plans were infiltrated by their coming together. If he and I made plans for our church services, he would change them to what he and she devised. Our first New Year's Eve service was an example of that:

(Episode 3) He and I planned to have a special New Year's Eve service. Together they decided to have a fun night in her apartment instead. Her sons did not want to go to church and she wanted to be home with them in bringing in the new year. He said that he did not want to have service without her, so they decided not to have the service and just have fun. I did not agree; however, it did not matter. That evening, I came home from work sick. I had the flu. I was weak, had a fever, my body ached and my chest and head were seriously burning from congestion. Without any care or concern from him, I had to go to the store to get some flu medicine. He didn't pray for me, massage me, say he hoped I felt better. He said nothing but, "I am going to her place early while she sets up." When I arrived, the room was small and pretty full. They had already begun their program. My husband was in a chair next to her while she was sitting at the end of the sofa. Together they looked at me when I entered the room, looking for a seat. He never greeted me or acknowledged that I was there. He just kept talking. Neither one of them offered me a chair. I found a chair in the kitchen.

Not feeling well, I sat at the kitchen table and rested my head on my arms. I could hear him talk. The "First Lady," "Co-pastor," Pastor Robin, whoever I was supposed to be, was sitting on the outside never once checked on or invited in. Again, this was their norm but my disgrace. He canceled our church service because he did not want to do it without her, but it was no problem for him to do this event without me. Her sons weren't with her for the entire evening. I was not surprised; I had become accustomed to the twists and lies. Later at home when I mentioned how disrespected I felt, his only response was that no one had assigned seats. I told him, "A gentleman and a loving spouse would have offered his seat and made sure his wife was included." There is no other place other than the *Twilight Zone* that his actions would seem right. In Christ we do not slip into the *Twilight Zone.* It is outside of Christ that these episodes happen. No matter how many scriptures we know or our religious title, we are not exempt from slipping into the *Twilight Zone* if we stop loving, caring, and nurturing our relationship with our spouse.

(Episode 4) Last but not least, our home seemed like a second home because he found many reasons to spend much time in her apartment. She lived directly beneath us. Just about every morning on my scheduled day off, I would wake up and he would be gone. I would get dressed and go straight down to her apartment. Each time, I would find him there. Several times, she would still be in her night garments. He was comfortably sitting at her table with her in her night clothes. I never felt good about that. In my presence, she cinched her robe. I could not help but wonder if that robe was cinched outside of my presence. One time I asked him what was he doing as she was inappropriately dressed. He agitatedly replied that he was just talking.

Despite the fact that I cooked, many times he would sit at her table and eat her food and take my food to work for lunch. He asked her to run errands and all sorts of things for him. He would go to work, go to sleep and then the rest of his free time was with her. It was an ungodly, awkward feeling of being married to a man who openly gave that type attention to another woman. It is bad when things are done behind your back but it is ten times worse when things are done in your face. It is one hundred times worse when your husband is a pastor. However, these bizarre, physiological twists of reality are just fine in the space and time of the *Twilight Zone.*

It is delusional to think that we can live out our immoral lusts in a holy marriage. Trying to force a wrong into a right will never equal right. It is my opinion that marriage is the best institution in the world. It is one of the components that keeps our society civil. Let's keep it preserved and do all that we can do to stay out of the *Twilight Zone.*

Click Zone

If not careful, we could violate one principle after another in our marriage and cause things to get chaotic. We should take the time to learn God's principles regarding marriage. A healthy marriage is a marriage in which communication is unhindered, consideration is always demonstrated, respect is given and the expression of love covers a multitude of faults. If your spouse is recklessly violating these principles, ask the Lord with all diligence to help you sanely go through this particular phase. Ask God to help you not to go into the *Click Zone.* It is in that zone that we are provoked to do some temporarily insane things. It is where crimes of passion are committed. Many spouses are dead or are spending time in prison because of this zone.

When slipping into the *Click Zone* it is like scenes in the movies when the eyes dilate and loud jungle-related noises (bongos beating rapidly, monkeys screeching, elephants trumpeting) play just before some serious damage is done. I am familiar with the *Click Zone*. During one unbelievable night, I contemplated murder. I know now what it feels like to be at the brink of killing someone. I could literally feel demonic forces egging me on. I thank God that his angels were right there to help me hold my peace. I know that the angels were there because, I, Robin . . . Pastor Robin . . . entered the *Click Zone.*

We were planning to go to a ministry conference at a church in Florida. In preparation, she called me and told me that the women of the church were getting together to help the pastor and me with the things that we might like to eat on the long van ride to Florida. She asked me to write a separate list of the things I wanted and those that he wanted. I was surprise that she was offering to do something so nice for me, and I have to say I was a little suspicious. I know now my suspicion was God giving me a "heads up" for what was to come.

The night of travel, they loaded the van, and he made sure to position her up front for him to see her. I sat directly behind him, and we set out on our way. At one point, people began to open their bags to eat things. I noticed that no one was offering me the things they had promised, so I asked for my things. She said boldly and confidently, "Oh, no, Pastor Robin, we did not get you anything because we could not afford it." The things I had asked for came to less than $22.00. I asked if she was serious and received a reply of yes. "So when was I going to get a phone call to inform me of this change of decision?" I asked. She said, "We figured you went to the store sometime today to get your own stuff." I told them, "I would have if I had known the people who promised to do it weren't going to." I did not get so much as a piece of fruit or a twenty-five-cent bag of chips. Nothing.

I knew that he was privy to what was being said as he sat quietly. He showed no emotion concerning their breach of promise, inconveniencing his wife/pastor, and he made no effort to make sure I was okay. With her final bold "we could not afford it" statement, I looked at where he was sitting and noticed *his* items were all there. With his things at his fingertips a few minutes later, she said to him, subtly, "Pastor, do you want your peanuts (she had bought them for him)?" He gently replied, "No, Nee Nee, not right now." That was the straw that broke the camel's back. I clicked into the *Click Zone*. I saw my strong, muscular leg kicking his head through the windshield as he drove. I vividly saw blood. Without thought, I was positioning myself to lift my leg to kick him. Miraculously I heard God's voice in the midst of it all, saying, "Peace, be still. That is what they want you to do so they are justified in their actions." It had to be God's angels restraining me. My leg was literally shaking from an adrenaline rush.

He was fine that I did not have anything. He was fine that she had lied to me. That was very cruel, disrespectful, demeaning and so much more. When we stopped to get gas, she bought a bag of chips and had the gall to toss the bag at me, asking, "Is this what you want?" She was empowered by him. If God had not spoken to me, some precious soul would have been hospitalized . . . or a body would have been in the morgue. I tossed it back to her and said, "No, thank you." She later admitted that he told her not to get my things and say she could not afford it. She told me it was going to be a group effort from the ladies in church, but she never asked them. She lied yet again at my expense. God sincerely helped me to sanely go through that trial. They were spared the storm brewing inside of me.

Things continued to escalate, and my cup was running over with the many violations of our marriage he was committing. Three other times I went into the *Click Zone* before we separated. He was being secretive and provocative when she texted him. I jumped on him on the sofa, trying to take his phone. He wanted to continue to drive her vehicle, and I grabbed him by the collar trying to stop him from walking away from me when I was trying to talk to him about it. I punched him in the ear when he insulted me regarding defrauding me. After that last blow-up, I knew something had to change. He made it obvious that his heart towards me had waxed cold. It was evident that he did not care how I felt about his relationship with her. The love, if he ever had any for me, had been replaced with something very dark. It was obvious that he had no intentions of stopping the actions that were hurting me. I was provoked, and I wanted to hurt him back. I knew that his mean, cruel, thoughtless, uncaring behavior had to change or someone was going to be a lame (or dead) son of a sea biscuit.

The *Click Zone* is not a pretty place to enter. This zone can be violent and murderous. I can only say God helped me through this awful phase. I only made it because of Him. If you are finding that your spouse's behavior is provocative and brazen, you need help. If you can get help, get it. If you cannot get help, you need to get out before it is too late. If you both still want to dwell together, let an authority concerning this matter bring you back together helped. Take your time before rushing into anything and let them help you remove those elements that would drive you into the *Click Zone*.

Acceptance and Moving On

Before we separated, I tried to give my husband and this woman the benefit of the doubt, but their out-of-order behavior kept piling up into a disgraceful mess. I tried to be a good representation of leadership by helping her spiritually as well as financially. I privately gave her my bonus money to help her and her boys. She pretended to be my friend but I never felt her sincerity. I would catch her in so many lies. I just chalked it up that she had a problem with lying. Outside of what they were doing in my face, the phone records proved she was secretly being my husband's companion.

Six months after our separation I received the phone records, which put all the pieces of the puzzle together. I called him and told him that I wanted a letter of apology from both of them. They both were in error and they both tried to deceive me. This type of behavior was done in secret, and they could no longer try to tell me that nothing was going on. He told me he was not giving me anything, and he is not going to tell her to give me anything. In a feeling of wrath, I told him that I was coming to the building that he and she founded together on

Sunday, and I guaranteed him that I would get an apology from the both of them during his church service, one way or another. I then abruptly hung up.

After I hung up, I cried in agony, blubbering like a child. It felt like my heart was hanging outside of my chest. I had never felt that level of hurt. In my mind I saw all sorts of destructive things being done by my hand. I was literally calculating what I was going to do in my hatred of my husband and his companion. I have a new respect for the song *It's a Thin Line Between Love and Hate*. I was going to do some damage. At that time the warm presence of God entered my room. His gentle voice said to me, "You are only thinking of doing those things to feel better about what was done." He then said, "You will *never* feel better about what was done." I then realized that going after them was not going to produce anything but more hurt and pain for myself, and I would still not feel better about what they did. God then said, "Leave it alone. Vengeance is mine." He then, with a gentle, kind, soothing voice said, "Let me heal you." He said it again, but this time it felt like a warm hand gently placed my ripped-out heart back into my chest. I stopped hurting and crying. I did not threaten to come after him or her ever again. I realized that my husband made his choice and that choice was between him and God. I had to remove myself from the situation, get completely healed, and take God's word to heart, accept the breach of my marriage contract, accept that the course of my life had been altered and move on. A word to the wise: when God gives you a personal word to live by, it is for life. Do not limit it to your immediate circumstance because more adversities are coming, and you will need every syllable of God's word to help you through them..

As I journeyed through the acceptance-and-move-on phase, more hurtful events were headed my way like a speeding locomotive hauling a ton of bricks. The bricks of accusations started hitting me with full force, one after another. Acts of infidelity were developing like film in a photo shop. During our separation, the confessions started rolling out. Unfortunately, all involved teenagers within a time span of ten years.

I had to suffer long when a teenager went to the police station and filled out a report against him. I had to suffer long when hearing what was kept hush-hush for years when a teenager told the leadership of our church in detail about his inappropriate advances. The accusation that hurt the most was when he and one of the youths were witnessed messing around in my home, right under my nose. I felt sick-to-my-stomach perplexed and humiliated, and many thoughts went through my mind. All the memories of my wholesome family were now forever tainted.

My self-esteem was affected. I felt like it was buried under a ton of bricks. The temptation to feel like a lesser person weighed heavily upon me. The temptation to think that something was wrong with me weighed heavily upon me. The temptation hit me to think that my child-bearing stretch marks and weight gain had made me damaged goods. However, many reminded me of my self-worth. They helped me to see that I am a beautiful black woman with gifts and talents in contrast to being an immature young girl. They brought to my remembrance that I am of a royal priesthood, ambassador and heir to the throne of a true and living God. Remembering who I was -- who I am -- helped me to cover my family in prayer. It made it easy for me to forgive him and release the matter to the Lord. If the accusations were true, and my husband has asked God to forgive him, I have accepted that God has forgiven him. Who am I to exalt myself above the heart of God?

I devoted twenty-six years of my life to him. I gave him more than half of my existence. My forgiving him freed me to move forward. I remember the phrase *One monkey don't stop the show*. In this case, the greatest *show* on earth is my life. I came to terms that my (*one monkey*) husband had altered the course of my life. I had to get that life back on course and make sure I did not stop living. I owed it to myself to stay on the right course with God and success. I had to purposely be happy in spite of these major transitions in my life.

Twenty-six years of marriage -- that's a lot of years to have to start all over. I realized that I had the rest of my life through eternity to live it up. I asked God, "What do I do now?" He told me to pick back up writing ***Urban Joy***. Thanks to my harsh realities, ***Urban Joy*** has been released to the world. Inspired by God to write has been an honor and a great humbling experience. It has helped me tremendously. My life is so much better for doing it.

I am aware that some who go through this experience of infidelity do not have such a fortunate outcome. Some people clock out mentally when their mate cheats. Some people commit suicide. Some people grow to be hard and cold. Others have even killed because of the betrayal. Surprisingly, some accept the infidelity and watch their spouse cheat year after year. Their love, trust and respect dies. They hold onto the title of being married, however, the life of the marriage is gone. Many live a closed, empty, lonely life after the marriage vows have been broken. My prayer is that this book will fall into the hands of those who are going through this. I pray that the words will strengthen their hearts to live. Live your life to the fullest. Life goes on. Do not let the actions of one person determine your destiny. You cannot make one person your life. You will crumble if you do. Christ is the rock. He should be our foundation.

We desperately need truth to anchor us through these types of storms of deception. We must forgive and ask for forgiveness. If someone cheats, that does not give us a license to do wrong deeds like fighting, being vengeful, killing, paying back by cheating, hating or hurting. We do not have a license to die on the inside. The only way out of this *alive* and *well* is to stay open to hear the voice of God as He tunnels you through. **Pray** and ask God to help you hear His voice. Ask God to remove any obstruction that will hinder you from hearing Him. Ask God to help you be attentive to and to appeal to His and only His instructions. It was God's voice that gave me the peace and joy of living. I thank God that during the times that I was ready to kill, He was right there to stop me. God was there to stop me from doing some life-changing damage. I am so grateful that I am not in jail; the girls still have their father, and I have forgiven him. My life is ninety times better than it was before. God's second is always better.

You will not appreciate the indiscretion unless you are looking for a way out. God will enable you to move on while knowing about the indiscretion. The wonderful thing about how we are created is that our hearts and minds have many chambers. It is amazing how Dr. Siegel discovered that we have the capability to "get ourselves off the autopilot of ingrained behavior." We can shut thoughts down in our minds and simultaneously rejoice. We have the privilege to cast whatever we are going through to the Lord because we are His personal concerns. Get this word picture in your mind. You are standing on the edge of a cliff, and the Lord is standing in the valley. Everything that you are going through is in a sack. Cast it to the Lord and *live*! Live every day to the fullest. Forgive, release and go on. Go in another direction in your mind. Your deeds will follow suit. I have come to the conclusion that infidelity in a relationship is not the worst thing that can happen to me. The circus of life has more than *one monkey.* Enjoy the rest of the circus without that *one monkey.* You will discover that there is so much more to enjoy. There are a lot of attractions. We may have to be patient to get through some of them. The important thing is to *enjoy the show.*

There are going to be a number of things you will have to process while you are transitioning forward. In Christ, He will take you through a healing process. You do not have to fall down on your face. You do not have to live like a victim, hurt and beaten down. You do not have to live in anger. You do not have to die on the inside. When my husband muttered out of his mouth, "Why don't you just leave? " God's still small voice said, "That is enough." I knew I needed a place to stay. The Lord would not let me run back home to daddy in NJ. I had to stay and work things out. I found a place in a week close to my job. I did not have a car and I had to walk. I had to process everything that I was going through and look to God to go through it successfully. I also had to heal properly.

Healing Process

A few months into our separation, while working I saw a couple gracefully walk through the dealership. The gentleman took his lady over to the vehicle that I wanted. As I watched them interact with each other, I could tell that he was gentle towards her. He was holding her hand like she was precious. I could tell that he really appreciated her presence. I became depressed when I saw that. It just showed me what I did not have. It reminded me of the rejection I suffered living with my husband. I could not concentrate. I asked to be excused. I gathered my things on my traveling cart, put on my tennis shoes and started walking. The more I walked the angrier I got. I was angry with God.

In your healing process, watch out for being angry with God. I said to God, "All that I have done for you is this what I get? I served you with all my heart, completely sold out and this is what I get? I see people living all kinds of lives and they are doing way better than I am." I said, "Maybe I need to go over to the other side." Before I could get the word "side" out completely, God said to me, "I did not do that to you", and again He said, "I did not do that to you. If you think that this trial is something living in me, what do you think it will be like living outside of Me? You are saying this because someone rejected you? You are saying this because your husband rejected you?" I immediately pictured Christ being rejected on the cross.

God said, “Don’t you know that there are women who are no longer on this earth because their husbands have not only rejected them but abused them and took their lives? Don’t you know that there are women whose husbands not only rejected them but have riddled their bodies with diseases that there is no cure? You are crying because you are walking. Look at your legs. Do you see how strong they are? Don’t you know that there are people right now in the hospital that cannot move at all? You are walking to a beautiful home. Right now there are people who are homeless. You are leaving a good job making good money. Right now there are people who are unemployed in need of a job. Your refrigerator and cupboards are full. Right now there are people who do not know where they are going to get their next meal.” He told me, “Start counting your blessings and start being thankful for what you do have.” The impression He left in my spirit was to dry it up. He told me, "Be patient and watch my salvation." I got a clean check in my heart to move forward.

Since that day, I have never had a conversation like that with Him again. I do not think that I need to be told twice. God set me straight. I have to say that I have done exactly that and I have never been this blessed in my entire life. He has been proving Himself to me over and over. I am so grateful. The Lord has a beautiful way of taking our minds off of the things that are not important or beneficial. *In your healing process allow God to put your mind on those things that are most needful in your life.* He took my mind off of the betrayal, rejection and neglect and put my mind on being grateful for all that I have and will have. He took my mind to a place of being grateful for all that I am and will be.

God knows how it feels. Man has been betraying Him since Adam and Eve. It is human nature to go after the forbidden. Do not keep reliving the fact that his or her attention went to someone else. Instead, relive the fact that Christ said that he will never leave us nor forsake us. That promise has to really mean something to you in order to be joy in this situation. Principles are violated in marriage every day; statistically adultery happens everywhere. From ministers to movie stars, no one is exempt. Get counseling and go on. Live your life. You only get one chance on earth to do it. If you can reconcile, then reconcile. I personally know couples who have stayed together after this type of ordeal. If you cannot reconcile (after counseling), then go on. Become skillful in departmentalizing your past, present and future in a way that you will flourish. John Maxwell quoted, “Cherish your yesterday, live your today and dream your tomorrow.” I say the things that you cannot cherish, put it under the blood of Christ and leave it there. The things that hinder you from enjoying your living today, cut them off. The thoughts that prevent you from dreaming, abandon.

Let God orchestrate your healing process. You will heal so much better. God told me to go see Pastor Robyn Gool. He is the senior minister of Victory Christian Center in Charlotte North Carolina. He is the founder of Victory Christian School. He is also known for his television program. At that time, I had never been to his ministry. I had never spoken with him personally. I took a step of faith and went and placed my life’s story in the hands of a man that I had never met. His advice is still bearing fruit in my life today. He instructed me to:

1) Focus on you. Care about you and your wellbeing.
2) Get financially established.
3) Keep your children encouraged as well as emotionally and spiritually stable.
4) Find a church where you can get spiritually nourished, built up and encouraged. Get your self-confidence and self-esteem restored in Christ first, before getting involved.
5) Do not go after your husband and try and fix your marriage. You have done all that you could do. The ball is now in his court.

I told Pastor Gool that I would like to come to his church to get more direction. He was kind enough to set up a ride for me. I will never forget Ms. Queen Ossie. She traveled far to get me. She is full of life. She kept me laughing and going until I was able to stand on my own. I thank her. I thank God for the both of them. They were key in my transitioning properly.

Pastor Gool promised to call my husband and offer his services. My husband did not accept Pastor Gool’s help; he never did anything to reconcile; he never ceased his relationship with the woman or with other women. I knew I had every right in the world and in God to divorce him. However, I needed to hear a word from the Lord before I would make things final. Only God knows a man’s heart. I knew that only God would know if he would make things right with us or he would continue that path that he was on. So I waited.

My spouse decided that divorce was best. In the state of North

Carolina it only takes one to file for divorce and it would be granted. He called me one day in the morning around ten a.m. and told me casually that I should be receiving divorce papers in the mail soon. I asked him was he sure and he said, "Yes, I think that it would be best." I asked again and he repeated his answer. He was involved with another woman. I said okay. I must tell you that it was not okay in my heart. In that moment, after two years of separation, I came face-to-face with the reality that he did not cherish the beauty of our family like I did and that he was really done. Within two weeks, an officer came to my job to serve me divorce papers in front of everyone.

I wanted a better exit. I felt that I deserved a better cloture. However, when I was crying to my daughter she said that he was not capable of giving me a better cloture. She said that if he was, I would have gotten it. She asked me, "Why do you think it is wrong to let dad go?" She said, "Let him go!" I had to go to God because I knew that He would be the only one to get me through this emotional trial. I lay before him. I really did not have any more words to pray. I prayed all that I could pray about the matter for years. I just needed to lie before Him.

In your healing process be careful of delivering yourself. Wait on God to deliver you. As I was lying before Him crying, He did not speak to me right away. Eventually God said, "*Why do you look at second like it is not good?*" It was a peculiar question, but in my heart I knew what He was asking me. I felt compelled to answer, "Well it is like being in a beauty pageant and winning first runner-up. I was good but just not good enough to win the crown. It feels like I have failed." I then told God, "You told me to marry him. You are not fickle. I feel that if I think or do anything different, I am going against you." God then asked me, "Well, what do you think about my son, He is the second Adam?" When God said that it felt like menthol filled my mind. Immediately, I had a paradigm shift about second. I said, "Well, I love Him. I think that He is awesome and, great!"

He then said, "Robin, in life everything has to die." When God said that to me, what came to my mind was ***Ecclesiastes 4.*** In that chapter it says, "There is a season for everything, a season to live and a season to die...." God then instructed me to look on my patio at the bouquet of flowers in my hanging baskets. They were full of color and beautiful. He said, "Don't you know that every flower that you see there was a seed that had to die in order to produce that beautiful bouquet of flowers?" I knew right then that God was saying it's okay to release my husband and let him go. Let the marriage die and I would see my life blossom like a beautiful bouquet of flowers. When that revelation came, I stopped crying. He then said in sort of a sarcastic tone, "So what do you think about my second coming, do you have a problem with that?" I laughed. I answered by saying, no, and then smiled. I have been smiling ever since. It was very uncomfortable to wait on God. But I did and He freed me, blessed me, loved me, comforted me and gave me hope and great expectation for what is to come.

I shared the revelation that God had given me about Christ being the second Adam in conjunction of what I was going through to a pastor that I knew. He affirmed that the revelation was from God. He said, "I am sure you would say that it was God that put the two of you together." I said, "Yes." He said, "It was God that created Adam. However, when Adam sinned, God sent a substitute. Throughout the *Bible*, people altered the plan of God, and God sent a substitute; the substitute would always be better." Just know that if you find yourself in this situation, whether you stay with your spouse or whether you get a divorce, let the Lord guide you all the way, because he always has something greater in store for your life. ***Jeremiah 29:11***(KJV) says, "For I know the thoughts that I think toward you, saith the lord, thoughts of peace, and not of evil, to give you an expected end."

In your healing process, stay in the passenger seat and watch God orchestrate an awesome expected end. The joy of knowing that God is there to deliver me is priceless. The joy of knowing that He is making my life as beautiful as a bouquet of flowers strengthens me. That personal word stirred my expectation. In this situation, God has a personal word for you, too.

Whatever personal word God has for you, just trust him and follow His precise plan. We also have to exercise our patience while waiting for our deliverance. **Pray** and ask God to help you forgive and release the offense of your cheating spouse. Ask God to help you successfully get through the healing process. Ask God to minute-by-minute help you regain your joy of living. The joy of living is a benefit while waiting. Living ***Urban Joy*** is God's way of exercising vengeance, and it sweetly implodes the bitter pain of being married to a cheater.

~ On the Wings of Devastation in the Arms of the Lord~

In my life I have seen much devastation. I have seen people lose everything because of a catastrophe. The magnitude of loss felt from the death of family members, wives, husbands and children is tremendous. Many have taken years to build their lives, then in a moment a strong wind, flood, mud, snow and or fire would sweep through and wipe out everything. To many, it is a conundrum of the world that only God knows the answer. Many have said and wondered, “Why has God allowed this devastation?” Many have said "Where was God in all of this?" Some have concluded that there is no God due to the tremendous loss, pain and suffering. In all of my studies, I have learned that there truly is nothing new under the sun. Catastrophic events journey as far back as before the birth of creation. It is human nature to blame someone or something when things go wrong. It is also human nature to blame God when a natural disaster occurs.

Catastrophic events are a harsh reality of life. It is the “ugly” in our world that no one wants to see. When these events happen, it is not life or God carrying out a personal vendetta against us. It is just very unfortunate. Finding fault is fruitless. We never get any further by finding fault. What is needed during times like this isn’t finding fault, but finding in our hearts the acts of compassion and kindness for mankind. We should band together and intelligently bring back to order the infrastructure of society. Our hearts shouldn’t turn away from God; we should nestle into His arms. We should look to the one who is greater than life. We must turn to God for his strength and comfort in order to get through the devastation. We need the inner peace and joy to survive wholly (mind, soul and body). We need to free our minds of fault and blame in order to think on the things that will preserve the values, memories and traditions of our people. We are left behind to pick up the pieces and to rebuild. The building process will of a certainty take place because it is a natural phenomenon. In this situation we could do two things, enjoy the rebuilding process or not enjoy the process. It is totally up to us.

A peace of mind and a heart of joy hold more substance, stability, and strength than self-pity, grief, misery and blame.

Looking to a God that you cannot see takes strong faith. Faith is not a natural instinct, it is given by God. ***Romans 12:3*** (KJV) says, "… To every man that is among you, not to think of himself more highly than he ought to think; but think soberly, according as God has dealt to every man the measure of faith." Blaming God for something that we are not sure He has done is not sober thinking. We are thinking higher than we ought when we say things of a certainty with no proof, just assumption. I surmise that we think a catastrophe is an act of God because it is beyond our comprehension. So, who better to pin it on but a deity that is beyond our comprehension?

The faith that God has dealt to everyone gives us the ability to trust that He will get us through the hardship. We rarely trust anyone that we do not know. We will not trust God if we do not know Him. Having a relationship with God increases our level of trust in Him. ***(Romans 10:9-10).*** Once the relationship has been established, ***Romans 10:17*** (KJV) comes into play, "So then faith comes by hearing and hearing by the word of God." The investment of time together is pertinent. The word of God will become alive to us and we will develop the hindsight and foresight needed. It will be nothing for us to believe in ***Psalms 91:1***(KJV) "He that dwells in the secret place of the most high will abide under the shadow of the Almighty."

Abiding under the shadow of the Almighty is a comforting thought. If we die, we will be with Him. If we live, we thank Him for the life that we have in Him. If we lose everything, we trust that all that has been lost, God will restore. Time and time again, we have seen cities, towns, homes and families restored. ***Psalms 51:12,*** David prayed to God asking Him to restore the joy of his salvation and the latter of the scripture he prays, "...and uphold me with thy free spirit." **Pray** and ask God to restore within you the joy of your salvation and uphold within you a right spirit. David knew how it felt to lose everything. A free-spirited person is a joyful person. Being upheld by God's free spirit is void of the weight and problems of the world. It makes the rebuilding process so much better.

Trusting God and fortifying ourselves with His word breeds champions, not losers. One may say, "I have lost everything, how am I a champion?" You have won the battle of life over death. You are alive! The greatest thing that you have not lost is God, the hope of His promises and the joy of your salvation. Enjoy your life, champion. "You live longer once you realize that any time spent being unhappy is wasted." -- Ruth E. Renkel, author and poet. Start all over with new aspirations in your heart. It is a waste of life to live any other way. "We cannot waste time. We can only waste ourselves." -- George M. Adams, political figure in the 1800's. In the *Bible,* Job was wealthier than we could imagine. On the wings of devastation, he lost his family, health and all of his possessions. God restored back to Job everything and more. Every bird that flies must land. Some land in the mouth of death and devastation and others land in a safe haven. In Christ, whether we are flying on the wings of devastation or into a safe haven, we will always land in the arms of the Lord. There is nothing greater than being held by our creator during harsh times.

Thank you for reading this book. I hope that in some way I have helped, encouraged and blessed you. Please let me know how this book has impacted your life. Let me know if you were encouraged and motivated to be joy always.

My email address is rmedley-israel@joyotlenterprises.org. I leave you with these final thoughts; Enjoy your life today for tomorrow is not promised. ***Psalm 118:24*** (KJV) should be our daily confession, "This is the day which the Lord hath made; we will rejoice and be glad in it."

"And in the end, it's not the years in your life that count. It's the life in your years."

-- Abraham Lincoln

~ Study Guide~

Proverbs 10:15 "A rich man's wealth is his strong city"
Matthew 6:21 "For where your treasure is, there will your heart be also"

Urban Joy (*ur'ben – joi*) 1. Of, relating to or the characteristic of joy. 2. Being enriched with joy which governs our entire being as a strong city. 3. Joy serving as a magistrate administering it's power to flow through the city of a person's heart into the veins of their existence in the midst of pain, suffering, adversity, trials and or tribulations.

Joy is our inheritance from God. God's word is the resource that aids us in living out a joyful life while facing tribulations. Pull out your *Bible* and study the scriptures. Saturate your mind with them. You will love the person that you are.

Romans 14:17 – Kingdom of God..... righteousness, peace and joy...

St. John 16:24 – .... fullness of joy

Nehemiah 8:10 – joy .... is your strength

Psalms 127:4-5 – ... joyful are we who have children

Psalms 30:5 – Weeping ... but joy comes in the morning

Proverbs 17:22 – A merry heart does good like a medicine...

Luke 2:10 – ... to know Jesus great joy is for all

Galatians 5:22 – ... fruit of the Spirit is love, JOY..

Proverbs 17:22 – A merry heart does good like a medicine

James 1:2 – Count it all joy when you fall into diverse temptations.

Philippians 4:4– Rejoice in the Lord always and again I say rejoice

I Thessalonians – 5:16, Rejoice ever more

I Peter 1:7 – Rejoice with joy unspeakable full of His glory

Ecclesiastes 2:26 – God promises to give ... wisdom, knowledge and joy

Proverbs 19:10 – Delight is not seemly for a fool

Psalms 37:4 – Delight yourself··· He will give you the desires of your heart.”

~Words of Thanks~

It took a total of six years before I sent this book to the publisher. This book transitioned as my life transitioned. Special thanks go to Graphics Designer Myke Etheredge and Editor/Publisher Lee Clevenger, along with daughters Angela Witt and Stephenie Chatman; Melissa Walters; Glenda Vaughn; Cindy Witt; Felicia Buchannan, and Pastor Annie Fields.

Cover design by:

iffective media ink

Rated I for Iffective

CPSIA information can be obtained at www.ICGtesting.com
Printed in the USA
BVOW02s0414191113

336666BV00002B/3/P

9 780985 925574